Pathways to Serenity

Philip St. Romain

LIGUORI
PUBLICATIONS

One Liguori Drive
Liguori, Missouri 63057
(314) 464-2500

Imprimi Potest:
Stephen T. Palmer, C.SS.R.
Provincial, St. Louis Province
The Redemptorists

Imprimatur:
Monsignor Maurice F. Byrne
Vice Chancellor, Archdiocese of St. Louis

ISBN 0-89243-289-6
Library of Congress Catalog Card Number: 88-80664

Cover photo by H. Armstrong Roberts

Contents

PART THREE
Appendixes

Introduction

The one word which impresses me as the most desirable state of being is *serenity*. It is true that joy and happiness are also wonderful experiences, but it is doubtful that even these states have any meaning without serenity.

The experience of serenity seems rather difficult to describe. I have often asked individuals in groups and workshops to specify their experiences of serenity and, as might be expected, they report peace of mind as a first characteristic. Many also mention a sense of being completely at ease with themselves in life. Some express an experience of unity with all creation and all of time; others say it is a feeling that all is well with the universe. Webster's definition of the word *serene* seems to summarize their responses: serene, *adj.* "Clear and free of storms or unpleasant change; shining bright and steady; marked by utter calm."

Despite the obvious desirability of the state of serenity, most of the people I know do not claim to experience serenity more than fifty percent of the time. Many have even come to doubt that they will ever experience serenity in this life! Just as there is general agreement concerning the experience of serenity, so, too, have these groups readily acknowledged the primary enemies of serenity. At the top of the list is fear — of death, of rejection by others, of the future, of economic failure, of the nuclear arms race, of suffering, of the loss of loved ones, and so forth. Most agree that fear and serenity cannot coexist for very long. Next on the list is a link between resentment and guilt — toward anyone and anything. Resentment, guilt, and fear seem to feed on each other, producing great misery in human lives. Other enemies of serenity are envy, low self-worth, sickness, unemployment, intoxication from mood-changing chemicals, stress — in short: matters of emotional pain. Where there is emotional pain, it is difficult to find serenity.

It is encouraging to me that serenity is a very firm promise which Christ guarantees his followers (see John 14:27). He also promises persecution in John 15:20, but it is understood that the persecution of the world cannot negate his peace, which surpasses all understanding. How sad that so few Christians experience the confirmation of this promise more than fifty percent of the time! Why should this be?

My own belief, which forms the basis of this book, is that people do not experience the peace of Christ because they do not live fully in the kingdom of God. They have not completely surrendered themselves to God, and consequently they experience emotional pain and selfish desires. This relationship between emotional pain and selfishness has become increasingly clear to me through my years of ministry as a counselor and teacher. Because people experience emotional pain, they naturally view the world through self-protective lenses. But this only leads to selfish behavior, which in turn adds more emotional pain to their inner turmoil. And so they plod along in pain and defensive self-interest, their hearts all the while longing for the serenity which they were created to experience as their "normal" state of being. What is needed today is a spirituality which can help people to break out of this addictive cycle of emotional pain and selfishness and refocus completely on kingdom living. Outlining such a spirituality is the concern of this book.

My Search for a Spirituality

During the past fifteen years I have searched throughout the Church for a balanced approach to fellowship with Jesus Christ. My adult search began with the Cursillo Movement, which was succeeded by the Charismatic Renewal. These two movements opened my spiritual eyes and taught me to pray, but after awhile I seemed to lose balance; I felt my growth in several areas was being stifled. I next approached the great spiritualities in the Church (Jesuit, Franciscan, Carmelite, Dominican, Redemptorist, among others). Having opted for marriage and fatherhood, I could not participate fully in the life of these communities. I could (and did) pray and study with them; I also attended retreats with these communities and went so far as to join a lay branch of one of them. Fruitful though these experiences were, I inevitably found it too strained a task to transplant these glorious spiritualities into the realm of the laity.

For a few years I floundered, persisting in prayer, Eucharist, and study, but I found no real spirituality to which I could commit myself completely. I participated in Scripture study groups, the RENEW Program, and joined various kinds of Church committees, but my growth seemed out of focus. All of these experiences were very helpful in different ways, and I highly recommend them all. But what was lacking was a spirituality — a structured approach to growth — to help me recognize and affirm the good in these activities while also pointing out other areas of growth.

Because of my work with substance abusers, I inevitably became familiar with the Twelve Steps of Alcoholics Anonymous. In the Twelve Steps I discovered a process for ongoing growth and an overarching structure to help me understand the meaning of my different growth experiences. I wrote of what I learned in *Becoming a New Person: Twelve Steps to Christian Growth* published by Liguori Publications, 1984. These Steps form an important backdrop to this book and are referred to in several places as disciplines for transformation.

Curiously, it was not until I began studying Buddhism and Zen that I came to see just why the Twelve Steps were so helpful. In the first place, most people working the Twelve Steps did so as members of a support group. This in itself is conducive to healing. Twelve Step groups allow people living in pain to meet others like themselves and so begin to form community. When a person walks into a Twelve Step group, he or she is essentially saying: "I'm screwed up, brothers and sisters, and I need you to help me get well." But the Twelve Steps don't just leave people wallowing in pain; they also provide a process for moving out of pain and selfishness to high-level wellness. It is no wonder that authors of such stature as M. Scott Peck have called Twelve Step groups the most important spiritual happening of the twentieth century.

I began to wonder if helping people move beyond pain was not also something the Church should be about. What does the Church provide for people to help them break out of the emotional pain caused by the selfishness of sin? My general impression is that most lay people (and many religious, too) lack a spirituality which helps them to move beyond pain toward healing and transformation in Christ.

To be sure, there is a great flurry of activity in the Church today — prayer meetings, Bible studies, collaborative ministry efforts, faith-sharing groups, and so forth. But what is being offered to help people put all this together? And what is being done to help people move beyond pain and selfishness? It seems that the sacrament of Penance with its new emphasis on reconciliation is still not sufficient in itself to meet this need.

I like the two essential ingredients behind the success of Twelve Step groups: (1) They provide an environment where people can come together in their pain, and (2) they offer a spirituality to help people move beyond pain. These two ingredients, I believe, are essential for any quality transformation. Unhappily, I find most Christian communities to be extremely deficient in both areas. The best example of a program that offers a safe environment where pains can be discussed is in a faith-sharing group like RENEW. But the heavy emphasis on Scripture, theological discussion, and ''storytelling'' in this and other similar groups keeps people at a safe distance from sharing their crosses with one another. Also, they do not provide a plan like the Twelve Steps to help people in these groups move beyond their pain to serenity.

At first I thought a solution to this need would be to form Christian Twelve-Step groups. I soon learned, however, that the Twelve Steps do not transplant very well outside of their communities of recovery. As a process for overcoming compulsive behaviors, they are unsurpassed. But as a spirituality for non-addicted ''healthy'' folk, they are difficult to grasp. I have also come to see that the Steps are lacking in several important areas which I believe to be essential for an authentic and holistic spirituality — areas such as the right use of feelings, discernment, and interpersonal skills. Given these difficulties in using the Twelve Steps, I began to see that other pathways will be needed to help people come to serenity.

Structure of This Book

What I shall attempt to do in this book is to outline a spirituality which, like the Twelve Steps, can help anyone to move beyond emotional pain and selfishness to a life of serenity centered in Christ. For this to happen there is a need to grow in seven spiritual living skill areas, which are presented in Part Two of this book. This approach represents a synthesis of basic psychological, ethical, and mystical principles, which mutually support one another. It incorporates principles found in the Twelve Steps, Christian Zen, and most of the great religious spiritualities of the Church. But remember: An effective spirituality is only one half of the equation for transformation; the other half is a support community in which participants use these principles. I have utilized this approach in my own support group and have found that it works very well.

The book is divided into three parts. Part One describes the framework within which human growth unfolds by examining the interaction between the activities of consciousness, human needs, ego states, and morality. This section helps to identify just what, precisely, a spirituality is supposed to do: namely, transform the whole of human consciousness in Christ. Part Two picks up this theme by presenting the seven spiritual living skills which enable people to focus their lives completely in Christ. Part Two also includes reflection on the relationship between spiritual living skills and grace. Part Three contains five appendixes. One consists of a series of helpful spiritual practices. Two and Three provide abbreviated summaries of the principles for growth which underpin this work. Four outlines a format for a support group to use this approach — a dream which moves me deeply. Five presents notes on Christian Cosmic Consciousness — a topic about which there is much interest these days. Finally, a Suggested Reading section provides an annotated list of books that I have found helpful in formulating this spirituality.

Acknowledgments

This book represents a summary of so many different experiences that it would be impossible to acknowledge them all. As the description of my own search for a spirituality noted, a primary influence has been the Twelve Steps of self-help groups. My good friend, Benny McArdle, deserves the credit here for pointing me toward the Twelve Step groups. Another friend, Herman Schluter, who coordinates Evangelization efforts for the Diocese of Baton Rouge, has agonized with me many times over how something like Twelve Step groups might work in a Christian setting. Members of my own Christian support group helped in different ways to formulate this structure. My "New Perspectives" support group friends also helped me to appreciate the role of imagination in transformation. A retreat on Zen by Father Ben Wren, S.J., enabled me to view spirituality from an Eastern perspective and to deepen my experience of contemplative prayer. John S. Sylvest, who has been one of my spiritual sounding boards through the years, provided helpful feedback on the manuscript, as did Father John Edmunds, S.T. My wife, Lisa, has hung in there with me through spiritual dark nights and meanderings; her common-sense feedback has been most helpful.

Finally, I wish to thank my three children for providing the catalyst leading to my confrontation with my immense selfishness. They, more than anyone else, have forced me to deal with my own Shadow issues, and to struggle to put together a spirituality which would keep me one-half step ahead of despair. The fruit of this struggle has been most surprising — a new, childlike state of consciousness similar in many respects to that which they already enjoy as a matter of course.

PART ONE

Functions of Consciousness and Human Growth

1 | Functions of Consciousness

Ignorance of the functioning of consciousness prevents people from growing. What, then, is consciousness and how does it work?

Consciousness, according to Webster, is "awareness, especially of something within oneself; the state of being characterized by sensation, emotion, volition, and thought." Most philosophers would agree with this.

Consciousness has to do with awareness and the objects with which awareness is concerned. In contrast is the unconscious realm of the psyche. Little is known about the contents of the unconscious until they are revealed in dreams or other energies and symbols which emerge into consciousness for assimilation. This points up the fact that consciousness is the responsible realm of the psyche. It is in consciousness that the ego, or "Self in awareness," resides. Such words as "me" or "I" or "mine" usually refer to the ego.

The functions of consciousness can be described as follows:

1. **Perceiving** notes what comes into consciousness; it includes data from the senses, memory, intuition, and imagination.
2. **Considering** evaluates data in the light of beliefs and values.
3. **Feeling** reacts emotionally to data perceived and evaluated.
4. **Deciding** reviews alternatives presented and makes a choice.
5. **Behaving** acts on the above decision.

The relationship between each of these functions of consciousness is demonstrated in the following Figure.

FIGURE ONE
How Consciousness Functions

PERCEPTION

(Receives data from the senses,
memory, intuition, and imagination)

↓

CONSIDERATION

(Evaluates data in light of beliefs and values)

↓

FEELING

(Reacts emotionally to data perceived and evaluated)

↓

DECISION

(Reviews alternatives presented and makes a choice)

↓

BEHAVIOR

(Acts on above decision)

In reflecting on the above Figure, two points need to be remembered. First, this outline does not attempt to demonstrate the metaphysical alignments of the functions of the psyche. There does not seem to be very much general agreement among the various experts on this subject. This leads to the second point. The Figure attempts to demonstrate only the general (not absolute) *relationships* between the functions of consciousness. In that sense, it can be a helpful guide for pointing out specific areas where changes need to take place.

To demonstrate the relationships outlined on this Figure, reflect on a story told by Father John Powell in his book, *The Christian Vision*. A man came home drunk one night, only to observe a thirty-five-foot snake on his lawn. He became frightened, so he got a hoe and began chopping away. The next morning, he discovered that he'd chopped his garden hose into pieces.

Note the following points:

- If your senses and imagination tell you that a hose is a snake, then everything else that follows will respond to "snake."
- The man was afraid. Why? Look to Figure One, and you will see that perception + consideration produce feelings. His knowledge (or ignorance) of snakes and the value he placed on his safety produced fear. With different beliefs, he might have experienced excitement.
- He chopped up the snake. Why? Because that's the option he *chose* for expressing his fear and actualizing his values. He had other options, such as calling the police or simply letting the "snake" slither away.

This example describing the functions of consciousness points out the tremendous freedom which exists at the level of beliefs and decisions. The man was free to interpret the meaning of the snake event in a number of ways; he was also free to choose between a number of options for expressing his fear. It is true that conditioned thinking and decision-making habits (not to mention his drunkenness) probably restricted his *experience* of freedom, and this is a real problem. But the possibility of growing out of conditioned responses will be noted throughout this book.

A final observation has to do with perception. Since every-thing begins with perception, it is necessary to see things as they really are. Perceiving reality as it is requires openness and receptivity; the perceiver needs clear glasses, not tinted lenses. Such clarity of vision is another important aspect of spiritual growth, as will be seen.

Reflection/Discussion/Questions

1. Discuss Webster's definition of consciousness and reflect especially on the meaning of the word *volition*.

2. Do you always see things as they really are?

3. Figure One demonstrates the relationship between the different functions of consciousness. Reflect on how they influence your spiritual growth.

2 | The Ego

So often you hear people say, "The trouble with 'so-and-so' is he/she has too big an ego." Most people would be insulted if told that they had an ego. That is because the common usage of this term is still heavily influenced by religion — in particular, mysticism — which tends to use the term *ego* in reference to narcissism and selfishness. (This meaning of the term will be treated in the next chapter.)

Among behavioral scientists, however, *ego* is not a pejorative term. Ego refers to the volitional and organizational center of consciousness; it is not moral or immoral. Indeed, it is only because of the ego that people can choose to do good or bad. Many times the primary role of counseling is to strengthen a hurting and fractured ego so that it can begin to make choices in behalf of the good of the whole organism. This central role of the ego in consciousness is demonstrated on the next page.

FIGURE TWO
Role of the Ego in Consciousness

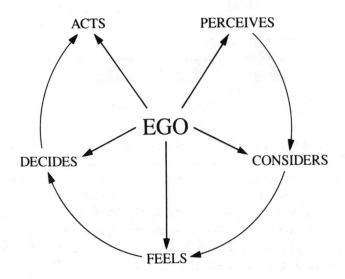

The two general attitudes of the ego are "I am," and "I want." These two attitudes bring about a sense of personal energy and identity — a sense of self (although the ego is not the whole self but only the self in the here and now). The "I am" attitude, which is simple awareness, may be directed toward any of the functions or anything within their sphere. For example, the ego might note, "I am feeling tired," noting its connection with feelings, or "I am reviewing my options," as when making a decision. When directing its gaze outside the psyche through the sensate functions, the ego awareness might say, "I am enjoying the smell of this flower and I see how its petals are a beautiful shade of lavender!" In this case, the flower, which enjoys an existence independent of the human psyche, has nonetheless been brought into the psyche through the ego's employment of the sensate function.

While ego awareness ("I am") is a relatively uncomplicated state, ego desiring ("I want") is another matter altogether. What the ego desires generally has to do with the fulfillment of human needs. If you are thirsty, this need breaks into the awareness of the ego and attempts to stimulate the ego to make a decision to bring water into the body. No problem there: You have a simple bodily need whose fulfillment the ego is capable of attaining (provided the resources exist). Other needs such as food, shelter, sleep, and warm clothing are also obvious concerns of the ego. To neglect these concerns is to jeopardize bodily health.

In addition to physical needs, the ego is also concerned with psychological gratification. The four most common areas of psychological concern are esteem, status, security (which is physical as well), and power. You can survive physically without gratifying these needs, but life will surely be less meaningful (a factor which will ultimately lessen physical stamina).

Although both ego awareness and ego desiring are concerned with a myriad of different issues throughout each day, their primary concerns seem to be directed in five directions, one, physical, the other four, psychological:

1. **Will-to-pleasure** is concerned with the gratification of bodily needs and wants. Pleasure, in this sense, is the emotional reward for the gratification of bodily needs and wants.

2. **Will-to-esteem** refers to self-estimation and includes the manner in which you meet your emotional needs (acceptance, affirmation, validation). Without a healthy self-concept, you become vulnerable to a vast array of emotional and physical ailments.

3. **Will-to-security** constitutes your perception of the trustworthiness of reality — your physical, social, spiritual, and inner reality. If you do not attain a basic sense of security, life will be a fearful prospect.

4. **Will-to-status** denotes how you think others perceive you and how you meet your need for a sense of belonging. You

need to know that other people value you in some way and that you are important to them.

5. **Will-to-power** indicates your experience of freedom and control. If you feel unfree and powerless, you can become despondent. Conversely, the conviction that you can direct your own life in such a manner as to meet your needs leads to hope.

Each of these five ego orientations is unique in its own right: Each has its own agenda. It is not uncommon, however, to find them blending with one another to produce complicated life goals. The will-to-status, for example, might be linked with economic prosperity (a security concern); power and wealth often go together, as do esteem and status. The peculiar blendings of ego orientations are unique for every person, but keeping the five primary orientations in mind can help you to sort through your own volitional issues.

Reflection/Discussion/Questions

1. Reflect on the differences between the common and the philosophical usage of the term *ego*.

2. What are the two general attitudes of the ego?

3. What are the physical needs of the human person? What are the psychological needs? Discuss them.

3 | The Small-self

"One man's castle is another man's hovel." This old saying suggests several important questions. How does the ego pursue the fulfillment of pleasure, esteem, security, status, and power? What are legitimate wants and needs in each of these areas? If one man's castle is another man's hovel, then why should this be? Why do some people want more than others? Why are some people never satisfied even though they have plenty?

To respond to these questions, recall the description of consciousness as the relationship between ego orientations and the functions of perceiving, considering, feeling, deciding, and behaving. What must now be added is another dimension: the motivational force behind these five functions.

A consciousness which draws its energy from fear, selfishness, and disunity is referred to as the small-self; one that feeds on the energy of love, unselfishness, and unity is called the

Christ-self — which will be treated in the next chapter. In Colossians 3:9-10, Saint Paul writes, "Stop lying to one another, since you have taken off the old self with its practices and have put on the new self, which is being renewed, for knowledge, in the image of its creator." Saint Paul's "old self" is equivalent to the small self because its orientation is very narrow and restrictive.

Since the energy that drives the small-self is fear, the small self is filled with anxiety with regard to the future and regret with regard to the past. It is fear and other pains which energize the small-self in its unrelenting concern with the words *me, my,* and *mine*. Such egocentricity leads to a distortion in the functions of consciousness.

The small-self views the world in terms of self-interest; thoughts, feelings, and decisions are made solely in response to egocentric concerns. In reference to the five basic areas of human need, this is what happens when the small-self acts:

1. **Will-to-pleasure** pursues food, drink, and sex in a distorted manner. The result is lust (sex for the sake of sex without reference to love) and gluttony (indulgence in food and drink for pleasure rather than bodily sustenance).

2. **Will-to-esteem** ignores God as its proper focus and ego becomes self-absorbed and proud. The consequences which follow will be either an extreme sense of independence manifested in narcissism and self-righteousness or extreme dependency manifested in low self-worth and shame.

3. **Will-to-security** attempts to overcome fear by accumulating goods (avariciousness) or by surrendering to fate and doing nothing (sloth). This can apply to a person's inner reality, relationships, and other areas of life in addition to the physical.

4. **Will-to-status** becomes corrupted through constant judgmental comparisons with others. This leads to envy (de-

siring what another possesses), pretentiousness (trying to impress people), and people-pleasing (doing what others want so as to be accepted by them).

5. **Will-to-power** attempts to control everything and everybody. Controllers try to manipulate others, either through subtle means or through threats of violence. Submissive types allow others to take control. In either case, the consequences often lead to resentment and violence.

Continuing indulgence in this manner only increases your disunity or separation from other people. You become like a cancer cell which has defined itself in relation to itself and not in relation to the needs of the body. In the small-self, there is suffering.

Another way of looking at the problems caused by the small-self is to see it in terms of what many mental health professionals are coming to recognize as the dependency process. You enter the dependency process any time you attempt to meet your basic needs by using people, things, and activities in an unhealthy manner. If this continues for a prolonged period, the dependency behaviors will become compulsive and abusive. Consciousness then becomes filled with guilt, shame, fear, anger, and loneliness. If these feelings are unresolved, the volitional center will ''collapse'' under their ''weight.'' Your psyche then becomes increasingly contaminated by these feelings, and your ego loses its power to direct the course of your life. This loss of willpower to break out of an unhealthy behavior pattern and the consequent unmanageability which results in your life is what is called addiction.

Addiction to food, drink, and mood-altering chemicals is entirely too common, but it is also possible to become addicted: to other things such as money; to people (co-dependency or addictive relationships); and to such activities as sex, gambling, working, shopping, and watching television. Many people manifest multiple addictions. Some of them become addicted to cocaine, sex, work, and gambling. After seeking help for their cocaine addiction — seemingly the deepest — their other addictions start to clear up. Later, however, these co-dependent tendencies begin to resurface. This is very typical. It is very likely that co-dependency is the most basic of all the addictions, generally resulting from poor upbringing in which people do not learn proper relationship skills and ways to meet their basic needs.

Addictions are clear examples of small-self consciousness; the deeper you move into the dependency process, the more addictions you will experience, and the more fearful, rigid, and unmanageable you will become.

But why all this misery? Since the small-self is so obviously an obstacle to happiness and the primary cause of global destruction, why should there be a small-self?

These questions constitute a major concern of religion. All religions recognize the problem of the small-self, although they do not necessarily use this terminology. Buddhism, for example, states that life is suffering, and it is the ignorant, craving, greedy self which is at the root of suffering. The Judeo-Christian-Islam tradition speaks of fallen human nature, or human sinfulness. Saint John indicates the dynamics of the small-self in his First Letter (4:18) which states: "There is no fear in love, but perfect love drives out fear because fear has to do with punishment, and so one who fears is not yet perfect in love." Fear is the psychological consequence of the absence of love. A consciousness which is not perfectly centered in love will therefore experience a certain amount of fear and, consequently, self-concern. With this understanding sin can be viewed as non-love; it is impossible to love in the small-self.

It is evident, however, that most of the people in this world do not live at either extreme: the small-self or the Christ-self. Most people stay clear of the extremes, but they are nonetheless constantly moving toward one or the other. "Life is an opportunity to become the kind of person you would like to be forever," reads an old adage. The small-self is one possible outcome, and one which should inspire you to constantly reflect upon the energies which motivate your becoming. That is why you must lay aside your former way of life and old self, which deteriorates through illusion and desire, and acquire a fresh, spiritual way of thinking.

Reflection/Discussion/Questions

1. In which of the five areas of need do you experience fear and selfishness most strongly?

2. Make a list of the consequences to yourself and others of your selfish behavior in each of the five areas of need.

3. What do you believe to be the ultimate roots of human selfishness?

4 | The Christ-self

The essential difference between the small-self and the Christ-self is that the latter is focused in love while the former is motivated by fear and selfishness. It is a matter of orientation. Learning to discern the energies which motivate you is one of the most important skills you need to cultivate for spiritual growth.

At the heart of the Christ-self is an ego which is centered in love. For a Christian, this center (or focus) is sharpened through faith in Jesus Christ as the Incarnation of Love itself. Jesus is the One who shows you how love perceives and thinks and behaves. Having such a model of love to stimulate the ego would be a great enough gift, but Christ does more than this. Because he is risen from the dead, Christ is now able to be in relationship with every living soul. His Holy Spirit is communicated directly into the soul; he is the mold in which human character is recast.

For many adults, the initial turning from the small-self to Christ happens as a powerful and dramatic shift in consciousness with deep feelings of love and joy. Such experiences are usually referred to as being "born-again," or saved. This experience might come within a retreat or at an altar call or within a period of sincere prayer. Whatever the catalyst, born-again people have no doubt that their lives have been turned around and that they are new people.

Although many people experience being born again, many others take a less dramatic route. For them, the spiritual journey is an ongoing process of conversion marked by many transforming experiences and many setbacks. Why some people have born-again experiences and others do not is a complicated issue. Temperament, upbringing, lifestyle, and evangelization methods all play an important role. (For those who are interested in pursuing this matter further, *The Varieties of Religious Experiences,* by William James, is highly recommended. This is a classic work, offering both enjoyable and educational reading material.)

Regardless of your route to conversion, living in the Christ-self calls for a transformation in all the functions of consciousness. Perceptions, beliefs, feelings, and decisions become responsive to the energies of love (the Holy Spirit) rather than fear. This will require a redefining of the manner in which you meet your five general needs. As Figure Three illustrates, the energies of love become incarnate through the practice of virtues. As you grow in the Christ-self, the fruits of such a life also become more visible. Contrast this with the profile of the small-self.

FIGURE THREE
Characteristics of the Small-self and the Christ-self

	Pleasure	Esteem	Security	Status	Power
The Small-self	Lust Gluttony	Pride Self-Righteousness Shame	Greed Sloth	Envy Pretentiousness Alienation	Anger Domination Violence Despair
The Christ-self	Chastity Moderation	Humility Modesty	Prudence Trust	Justice Service	Courage Patience

1. The **will-to-pleasure** becomes properly focused through the practicing of temperance, or moderation. You eat to live; you don't live just to eat. You enjoy sex as an expression of love and not just for physical stimulation. The result of such loving temperance is a healthy enjoyment of life's good things.

2. The **will-to-esteem** becomes properly focused by practicing the virtue of humility, or truthfulness about yourself. In the light of Christ's person, you see yourself as a child of God who is deeply loved, but who still has much growing to do. The result of this virtue is self-acceptance and self-knowledge.

3. The **will-to-security** becomes disciplined through the virtue of prudence. Prudence means that you make use of reason to plan for the securing of the necessities of life while leaving the rest in the hands of God. In time you come to trust that you shall have what you need when you need it.

4. The **will-to-status** becomes disciplined through service unto justice. In Christ, the greatest is the servant of all — a reversal of the worldly way. You undertake this service not to impress others but to further the kingdom of the Lord. Thus the spiritual results here are purity of heart and hope (for the victory that is sure to come).

5. The **will-to-power** is tamed through two seemingly contrary virtues: patience and courage. Patience means that you recognize your inability to control everything and everybody and your need for God in order to gain self-control. Courage means that you take the initiative to do what you can to change the things you can. The results of the Spirit here are self-control and assertiveness rooted in faith.

Growing in this Christ-self is, quite obviously, a lifelong project. Very few individuals have completely accomplished it in this life. For most persons, the project will be brought to completion in the hereafter.

Another obvious point is that so many people find it easier to make progress in some areas and harder in others. Most persons will struggle with pride and self-righteousness until they die, but some will struggle more than others. Some do not find envy a big struggle, but others do. Some, too, have a tough time with temperance and trust; others, however, take these in stride. Moving from small-self to Christ must take place in all areas of life, but your advances will proceed at different rates on different fronts. The gaps between strong and weak points cannot be too large, however. You are as strong as your greatest strengths, but as weak as your greatest weaknesses.

A final note on the Christ-self concerns those many people who are motivated by love and goodness, but who do not see Christ as the Lord of this journey. Many humanists, for example, are committed to the virtues described above, but they do not profess faith in Christ. What can be said about such people? Do they have a Christ-self? Here are two observations on this point.

- Since love is of God, and his lovers know him and live in him (see 1 John 4:7), it must be acknowledged that loving humanists are, actually, in touch with God. However, they cannot properly be called Christians since Christians are professed followers of Christ.

- The risen Christ touches all lives — even the lives of those who are not Christians. As the way to the Father, Christ is constantly calling all souls to himself. Furthermore, he is the one who is responsible for remaking humanity into a new race. Where you see love and goodness, you see the work of Christ. This is why several prominent theologians have suggested that all non-Christian people of goodwill are anonymous Christians: They are cooperating with Christ, even though they do not know it.

At this point some will ask why be a Christian? The answer is that those who do not accept Christ, but who nonetheless attempt to live by love and virtue, will surely hurt for their lack of faith. Knowing Christ as the Ground of your *self* and enjoying relationship with him through prayer makes a difference. Without faith in Christ, growth unto the fullness of your humanity is most difficult. With faith, however, you rest assured that your journey will not be in vain.

Reflection/Discussion/Questions

1. How do you experience your Christ-self? How do you experience Christ in others?

2. Has your growth been marked by born-again experiences?

3. With which of the areas of virtue do you struggle? Which comes easier for you?

4. How does the author answer the question: Why be a Christian?

5 | Stages of Spiritual Growth

Christian growth, as has been seen, centers your life in Christ and meets your basic needs in accordance with loving virtues. This movement opposes the movement of the small-self, which would have you meet your needs in a selfish manner. If you have grasped these concepts, much progress has already been made. There is, however, one more dimension to add to this framework. It has to do with ego states, or the various developmental manifestations of the ego through the years.

Recall that the two basic attitudes of the ego are awareness and desiring. Ego states refer to whole systems of awareness that influence the manner in which you attempt to meet your needs. Drawn from several different schools of human development, here are eight basic ego levels that you must grow through and learn to live with in your journey through the years. These states are listed below.

1. Undifferentiated state: The personality may be directed by instincts, or the energies of the unconscious. In this state the ego is fragmented and almost powerless to direct the activities of the psyche. In the case of babies, who are highly motivated by instinct, it may not even be correct to say that there is an ego. Addictions of any sort also render such persons vulnerable to unconscious impulses. "I want what I want" describes the stance of such people.

2. Child state: Researchers in human development have described several levels of ego development which take place between eighteen months to six years of age. During these early years, the child forms emotional convictions about life — convictions which are retained through later years of development. The child also includes possibilities for wonder, creativity, spontaneity, and fun. If, however, this inner child was abused or neglected, he or she pays the consequences in later life; if the child was properly nurtured, he or she will have more trust in life. For many, a primary task in spiritual development is healing the wounded child within. Its stance is, "I am little, and life is big and mysterious."

3. Parent state: This is the Freudian superego — a state of consciousness characterized by "shoulds," "musts," and "oughts." This state is programmed according to the manner in which your parents, teachers, and other authority figures treated you. It once played an essential role in helping you learn to discipline your instincts, but often sits on your shoulders as a spoiler during adulthood. "What should I do?" is its primary attitude.

4. Persona state: The Persona refers to the self you would like others to see. It is often called the Conformist state. Generally, this state is attuned to the expectations of others and becomes intensely manifest during adolescence — which is why the young are so vulnerable to peer pressure. Adults are also prone to wear masks and play games to impress others. Taking off these masks is an important goal in personal growth. "What will other people think of me?" describes the stance of such people.

5. Conscientious state: This state is characterized by internal motivation directed by goals. It has its roots in childhood fantasies, then becomes the adolescent's antidote to peer pressure and the young adult's center of career goals. Research indicates that few people move very far beyond the beginnings of realizing this state. "What's my goal?" or "What's right for me apart from the expectations of others?" is the stance here.

6. Shadow state: This is not so much a state as a part of self you do not want the world to see. Carl Jung called it the Shadow side, which usually is encountered in your late twenties. Generally it includes feelings and ideas about self and others that cause shame, embarrassment, resentment, and confusion. But it may also include positive energies that you are afraid to show. Given the right conditions (drunkenness, tiredness, therapy), the Shadow often asserts itself, much to the dismay of the person trying to hide it. "I don't know what came over me!" is what such people say in retrospect.

7. Adult state: Sometimes called the Compassionate state, this is the ego that has separated itself from parent, child, conventional and instinctual voices, and now serves as arbitrator among them. In this state is found a balanced internal locus for controlling behavior. "What is needed in this situation?" describes its stance. A full experience of the Adult state is contingent upon coming to terms with its Shadow state.

8. Cosmic state: The ego may lose itself in any activity during any period of growth. But what is meant here is a more or less permanent state in which the personality is no longer directed by a rigid, strictly controlled ego, but by a more universal level of the self. In such a state, you can say with Saint Paul, "I live, no longer I, but Christ Jesus lives in me" (Galatians 2:20). Many people experience this state for a short period of time; but only a few experience it as a permanent state of being. (See Appendix Four for a more detailed description of cosmic consciousness.)

To further your growth into the Christ-self, the following points about the above-mentioned ego states need to be underscored.

- With the exception of the Undifferentiated state, any state can serve as a medium for either love or selfishness. The Conscientious self may dream a dream rooted in love or fear; peer pressure may influence a healthy Persona state or an unhealthy one; Parent voices may communicate loving affirmation or shame.
- Through the years, your personal growth should bring the energies of the psyche under the control of the Adult state, which, in turn, should finally lose itself in Christ.
- Spiritual growth requires that you learn to discern the states out of which you are operating. This discernment is the prerogative of the Adult state, whose cultivation will be treated in Part Two.
- It is possible for you to move in and out of these states throughout each day. Indeed, it is possible (though certainly not desirable) to employ different states for the fulfillment of each of the five areas of need. For example, your will-to-pleasure may be directed largely by your Parent state; your esteem needs may emerge from your Child state; your status needs may flow from your Persona state; your security needs may arise from your Conscientious state; and your power needs may stem from a largely paranoid, instinctual base. In general, it can be said that most people live in a tension between three "adjacent" states (the Conscientious, Shadow, and Adult).

As you can see, your human growth is really a complex phenomenon. This is one reason why there should be no rigid interpretation of stage theories and personality profiles. As the Persona state indicates, it is possible to meet each of the five major areas of need by relying on different states. This makes for forty significantly different types of consciousness — already a fair level of diversity. If, in addition, you consider that each of these forty types of consciousness may be operating from one of the sixteen Myers-Briggs personality types, the result is 640 consciousness possibilities. Multiply this by the nine Enneagram types and you have 5,760 personalities — each of them unique. To really complicate things, you could factor in Kohlberg's six stages of moral development, Erickson's eight stages of social development, and Fowler's six stages of faith to come up with billions of different flavors of people, which is exactly what can be observed on the planet Earth.

People are all unique; they have to struggle to grow in the context of their own peculiar combinations of genetic energies, personal histories, and social environments. The one critical factor necessary for Christian growth calls for movement away from fear/selfishness/disunity toward love/unselfishness/unity. Eventually, this growth must be directed by the Adult state. But in the highest levels of spiritual growth, even this state must be relinquished as the ego becomes totally absorbed in Christ.

Reflection/Discussion/Questions

1. Which ego state do you most frequently utilize to meet your various needs? Use Figure Four (on next page) to make your response, enumerating your preferred state as number one, your second most preferred as number two, and so on. Do this for all five areas of need.

2. What sort of ideals were most important to you during adolescence and young adulthood? How have these changed?

3. How do you experience your Shadow state? Your Parent state? How do you make judgments among the different states in your adult life?

FIGURE FOUR
Basic Needs/Ego states Grid

States↓ Needs→	Pleasure	Esteem	Security	Status	Power
Cosmic					
Adult					
Shadow					
Conscientious					
Persona					
Parent					
Child					
Undifferentiated					

6 | Spirituality and Personal Growth

The approach to personal growth taken in this section is very basic and practical. All people have needs, and all use their functions of consciousness to define these needs and pursue their fulfillment. The key question, then, is how do you seek to meet your needs? Do you operate out of fear/selfishness/disunity or love/unselfishness/unity? These considerations will help you to root your spirituality in a sound psychology and solid ethics.

If you are like most people, you begin the journey to Christ-consciousness out of a combination of ego states and motives. Initially, you are a legion of consciousness, as you painfully discover when you come before God in silence. Your thoughts move in many directions, and it is hard to focus your attention on God. You must eventually move beyond this, for it is impossible to love very deeply when operating out of a fragmented consciousness. One of your most basic projects in spiritual growth, then, is to move toward living in the higher ego states. But this is not as easy as it sounds.

Moving from lower to higher ego states is a very natural trajectory in personal growth. As you grow older, consciousness expands and deepens to accommodate the variety and depth of your experiences. As Child you must learn to obey Parent voices; as an adolescent Persona you must break with the security of parental ties, and as a young adult you must break with convention to form your own ideals. Then you must confront the messier parts of life if you are to live peacefully as a balanced and whole Adult; and, finally, the Adult state itself must be transcended in Christ. Each transition period is marked by its own unique "dark nights" of pain and confusion. At each transition there is a sense of entering a strange new world in which you must learn, like newborn babies, to walk and talk all over again.

At the apex of development is the state of Cosmic Consciousness, in which the ego itself has become "softened" so that it easily transcends itself in love (see Appendix Five). This is the state after which you must yearn. You should intuitively know that you cannot find yourself unless you lose yourself, and that life lived too long in any of the lower ego states becomes too painful and stuffy.

The manner in which you lose yourself is a critical factor in personal growth, however. For example, alcohol and drug usage may very well represent an effort at Cosmic Consciousness. Getting high gives you an almost mystical sense of power and bliss; the ego can surrender its painful concerns for a while and be carried along by the experience. Unfortunately, this path to ego transcendence does not work, for the pain which was escaped only rears its ugly head again when the chemicals wear off. Therefore another chemical experience is sought, and so on it goes until, in the late stages of addiction, the result is not ego transcendence, but ego oblivion.

This brings up a very important principle: namely, that you cannot skip over growth states in order to live in the higher realms. If you attempt to do so, you will become neurotic. You must pay your dues! Counselors report cases of fifty-year-old adults who were still caught up in Parent and Persona levels; their next level of growth will be the Conscientious — even though they should have grown through this stage thirty years previously.

Here is another important observation: An overwhelming majority of people do not ever progress to life in the Adult state, much less the Cosmic state. Developmental researchers have noted that the usual level of development among adults is somewhere between the Persona and Conscientious states. The reason many people do not get much further is because they carry so much pain within — generally as a consequence of the dysfunctional situations in which they were raised. Their Child state is too dependent, their Parent voices too strict, their Persona preoccupations too limiting, and their Shadow state too dark for them to break out on their own into the freedom of the higher states. It is here that the partnership between psychology and religion is most significant. Psychology can help to heal the broken self through therapy; but religion provides the focus for self-integration — namely, God.

Lest you get the impression that what you have just read passes a negative judgment against those who have not (and will not, in this world) realized Cosmic Consciousness, it is necessary to remind yourself again that ego states and holiness are not necessarily correlated (except for Cosmic Consciousness, where you can't have one without the other). It is possible that persons in the Child state can be extremely loving and God-filled while Conscientious state people are often superbly qualified for wickedness. Recall that some of the most wicked people in history were extremely idealistic.

It is worth mentioning here, too, that religion itself often prevents growth into the higher realms. So many homilies seem to be addressing the Persona level — and that with a moralistic slant. In his thoroughly researched work on faith development, James Fowler noted that few preachers invite growth beyond the Conscientious level. Perhaps the language of sheep and shepherds has been taken a bit too literally here: to keep people in the Parent and Persona realms, treat them like sheep!

As mentioned in the Introduction to this book, Church leaders are woefully neglectful in helping people move through their Shadow times. Indeed, it seems much more likely that an agnostic humanist will reach the Adult state before a religious person. There has been so much unhealthy religion!

Sometimes religion actually contributes to the Shadow state by making people feel unduly shameful and burdened about problems they cannot control (as when alcoholics are denounced as sinners). Many Church leaders still operate out of a Parent type of religion, teaching "shoulds," "musts," and "oughts" about moral behavior. Yet the signs are everywhere that the overwhelming hungers among people today are for relief from pain and for mystical experience. These are the hungers manifest in present-day drug culture and in other movements such as Pentecostalism and New Age spirituality.

Aldous Huxley once wrote that the most certain sign of spiritual health in a culture can be seen in the percentage of contemplatives and mystics it produces. There can be no question that modern society is a miserable failure when evaluated according to this simple, yet profound, principle. If, as the developmental researchers maintain, Cosmic Consciousness represents the highest level of human development, then it follows that a culture ought to organize itself in such a manner as to help people grow into this state. Instead, it often seems that today's culture does the opposite by "forcing" people into roles and lifestyles that only increase their experiences of pain, egoic fragmentation, and social alienation.

Most people are burdened by incredible levels of stress and anxiety, and it is in such a state that they try to hold together marriages, to parent children, and to sustain other relationships. Happily, this is not the entire story; there are also many options for change and growth in today's culture. Yet there is no denying that those who are "on the way" represent a counter-cultural witness.

What, then, can be done to promote the fullness of human growth? The answer to that question takes matters quite a bit further than liberation theology and philosophies primarily concerned with economic and political justice. When the central focus is on the fullness of human growth, the inter-dependence of spirituality, political science, and sociology becomes apparent.

This leads to the next question: What is the work a spirituality must do to lead people to the fullness of growth? The answer is that a spirituality must help direct all of the functions of consciousness toward the ends for which they were created: to know, love, and serve God. Outlining such spiritual living skills will be the concern of Part Two.

Reflection/Discussion/Questions

1. Spiritual growth is primarily a movement toward a greater capacity to love. Do you agree with this statement? Explain.

2. How has religion helped you to grow in love? Or has religion retarded this growth in some way? Explain.

3. List some of the factors in today's society that mitigate against the fullness of growth. How do you cope with these issues?

4. How would you plot your own personal growth in the grid shown on the next page?

FIGURE FIVE
Personal Growth Trajectories

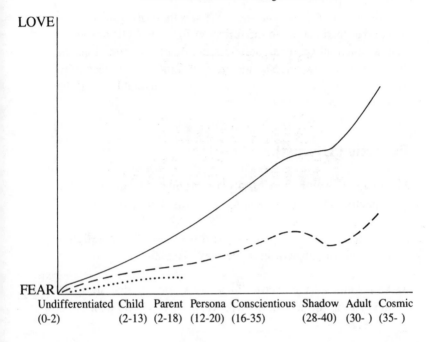

LOVE

FEAR

| Undifferentiated | Child | Parent | Persona | Conscientious | Shadow | Adult | Cosmic |
| (0-2) | (2-13) | (2-18) | (12-20) | (16-35) | (28-40) | (30-) | (35-) |

The vertical line represents growth in capacity to love, which is plotted against the horizontal line, representing transition through ego states (idealized age of duration is listed in parentheses). The solid line represents an ideal growth pattern, such as Christ's. The dotted line is that of a forty-year-old person who, for various reasons, never progresses beyond the Child-to-Parent state. The dash line represents the growth of a person who has reached the Adult state and is striving for the Cosmic state.

PART TWO

Spiritual
Living Skills

7 | A Basic Approach to Spirituality

Did you ever take classes on how to repair lawn mower engines? The instructor teaches the various parts of the engine, shows you how they were put together, and explains the contribution of each to the working of the whole system. If he is a good teacher, he will not only teach you about the parts but he will also give you the big picture of the relationships of the parts to the whole. You will come to understand how each part helps the engine to operate, and this relational knowledge will enable you to see the engine as a dynamic system rather than a mere collection of parts.

Human consciousness is also a great and powerful engine that you must learn to direct. It, too, has its many parts, and studying how these parts work together as a dynamic system is one of the most important lessons you can learn. Part One of this book described the operations of consciousness as perceiving, thinking (considering), feeling, and willing (deciding) — all of which produce behavior. The general movements of consciousness were described as various ego states responsive to fear and disunity (the small-self) or love and unity (the Christ-self). But Part One provided only a general sketch of the parts and movements of consciousness. This section and the next will attempt to fill in many of the details, but by no means all. The best that can be done is to provide an ''Owner's Manual'' of sorts that will enable you to better understand how your consciousness can be directed toward the realization of deeper levels of serenity.

The function of consciousness in the area of spirituality can be compared to the training undergone by long-distance runners. Your preparation to run in a marathon involves far more than simply jogging around each day. You must eat and sleep properly, wear the proper clothing and shoes, condition the muscles through stretch exercises, and so forth. Likewise, following Jesus will involve special training for each of the functions of consciousness. It is the goal of this section to describe the kind of spiritual training that is necessary to bring all of consciousness into the Christ life.

According to many, the skills necessary for living a spiritual life should be simplicity itself. ''All you need to do is love God and neighbor!'' they say. Others maintain that all that is necessary is to turn your life over to Christ and to let the Holy Spirit show the way. It is hard to argue with these approaches because, basically, they are correct. Also, the point is well-taken that the Scriptures emphasize faith in Jesus — and not in a particular spirituality — as the primary means for securing salvation. Indeed, Jesus refers to *himself* as the way to the Father (see John 14:6).

Yet there is no denying the existence of scriptural teachings concerning spiritual living skills. The early Church may well have regarded the risen Christ as the focus of salvation, but surrendering the functions of consciousness was another matter altogether. The Sermon on the Mount, for example, is as exhaustive a summary of spiritual living skills as will be found anywhere. That you must follow Jesus is obvious; the real question is *how* are you to do it — which is the primary concern of this section.

There is an urgent cry among God's people for a spirituality that enables them to grow in the fullness of Christian maturity. Here are some suggestions for a basic approach to spiritual growth — one that cannot be taken out of the context of all that follows in this section. It is being introduced at this point so that those who attempt to live this method will better appreciate all that follows.

This basic approach to spiritual growth emphasizes these disciplines: daily prayer; awareness, honesty, benevolence; and daily inventory.

Here is a brief examination of these factors.

Daily prayer: Very little progress can be made in your spiritual journey without prayer. In fact, most people eventually discover that all their spiritual living skills are a direct result of their prayer.

What kind of prayer should you practice?

You should practice the kind of prayer that has its focus in God, letting God love you while surrendering yourself to his will. This is the language used in Step 11 of the Twelve Steps of Alcoholics Anonymous, and it is also the formula in the Lord's Prayer. Prayer which has its focus in God enables you to experience the first of Jesus' two great commandments: to love the Lord with your whole heart, whole soul, whole mind, and whole strength. It is prayer that helps you to recognize the difference between your own will-to-self and your will-to-God. Learning to bring your own will into conformity with your will-to-God (or, rather, God's will-to-human) is the primary focus of spiritual growth, and prayer is your greatest ally in doing so.

Awareness, honesty, benevolence: These virtues are absolutely necessary for a basic approach to spirituality. They fulfill the second of Christ's two great commandments, "Love your neighbor as yourself."

Living in *awareness* means that you stay attuned to whatever it is you're doing. In short, you learn to live consciously instead of unconsciously. This awareness is accepted in a spirit of *honesty,* meaning that you acknowledge (at least to yourself) your perceptions, thoughts, feelings, and desires. Self-awareness of this sort leads to self-knowledge, a virtue that bears good fruit of its own. But awareness and honesty would be intolerable without *benevolence,* which means a compassionate regard for yourself, other people, and all of creation.

Each of these three virtues — awareness, honesty, and benevolence — must necessarily be shaped by the other two. Honesty and awareness without benevolence can be cruel and destructive; honesty and benevolence without awareness can be shallow and naïve; awareness and benevolence without honesty can be cheap and flattering. All three lived out together in a person of prayer will manifest to the world a beautiful example of human nature as it was intended to be.

Daily inventory: This third discipline requires that you take a few minutes at the end of each day to prayerfully reflect on how you have lived your day. You affirm the good you have done, and you honestly note the games you have played and the selfishness you have displayed. This is the time to ask for God's forgiveness and formulate strategies for dealing with areas of weakness. Those familiar with Redemptorist spirituality will recognize this as the examination of conscience held at the end of each day; in Twelve Step spirituality, this is Step 10. And in a similar vein, the focusing techniques of Dr. Eugene Gendlin make for a rich, holistic inventory.

Basic spirituality, then, requires daily prayer, living each day in awareness, honesty, and benevolence, and daily inventory. That these practices will produce spiritual growth there can be no doubt. And anyone who undertakes this basic approach will come to better appreciate the discussion of spiritual living skills that follow in the chapters ahead.

To learn these spiritual living skills, it is suggested that you work with one chapter each week and then repeat the process the following week. During your daily inventory, pay close atten-ticn to how you have practiced the skills you are studying that particular week. In doing this weekly and daily study, you will eventually form healthy habits based on the spiritual living skills.

If this recipe for growth sounds like hard work, then know that it is! It takes daily effort to move completely out of negative awareness. Yet is it not so that anything worthwhile in life generally requires struggle? The three essentials of change are: motivation, knowledge of skill areas, and practice. Your emotional pain and hunger for growth should provide ample motivation to change; this book outlines the necessary skills needed for growth; and the third ingredient — practice — depends entirely on you.

Practice, practice, practice: This is the secret of lasting growth. "No pain, no gain," reads another slogan seen frequently these days. What holds true for growth in other areas of life (athletics, relationships, career, and so forth) applies also for the cultivation of the Christ-self. It is through practice and prayer that you create good soil in your hearts that enables the Spirit of God to convert you into people of serenity.

The next seven chapters of this book will treat the actual living skills necessary for true growth in spirituality.

Reflection/Discussion/Questions

1. Reflect on the first six chapters of this book to make sure you understand the functions of consciousness.

2. Discuss the relationship between the functions of consciousness and your spiritual growth.

3. Why is the commandment to love God and neighbor not enough in itself to reach full Christian maturity?

4. Discuss the three disciplines so necessary for spiritual growth.

8 | Right Actions

Many people seem to think that religion and spirituality are primarily concerned with helping people to become moral. But it is entirely possible to behave morally — in a manner that builds up the human community — without being religious or spiritual at all. Religious people do not have a monopoly on ethics — not even on good ethics!

Actually, the relationship between morality and spirituality should be reversed. The reign of God that Jesus so often referred to is primarily a state of being-in-God. In this state, you behave morally — because actions follow from your state of being. In other words, spiritual growth will generally be accompanied by improvements in moral behavior; and, in the same vein, immoral behavior prevents spiritual growth — because being cannot advance when it is shackled by lower forms of behavior.

The point here is that conversion must advance in all areas of consciousness at once. Given the fact that there are different aspects of conversion, it is actually impossible to progress in one area without working on all of them. If you want right actions, you must also have right desires, right expression of feelings, right thoughts, and right awareness. It is likely that you will do better in some areas than in others, but no function of consciousness may be neglected for too long without limiting the development of your whole person. This holistic notion of conversion should be called to mind in any discussion of right actions.

What, then, is meant by right actions and what makes an action right or wrong?

For purposes of this discussion, right actions may be seen as those behaviors that generally help to build up the human community. Conversely, wrong actions are those that generally increase selfishness in the individual and that also hurt other people. Right actions increase love and wholeness; wrong actions increase emotional pain and separateness.

Most of the great religions of the world have provided teachings on right and wrong actions, and in this regard there is a strong convergence of opinion among them. Almost all agree that the following actions are generally wrong:

Killing. No religion allows for the arbitrary taking of life. Some religions sanction killing human beings in self-defense; others do not even sanction the killing of animals. Traditionally, Christianity has taken the former position, although many Christians claim that nonviolence is the ideal. Physical violence that has the aim of controlling others would also fall within the scope of this category.

Improper speech. This would include lying, gossiping, bragging, swearing, and other forms of loose speech that hurt others and distort the truth.

Stealing. This refers to both the taking of what belongs to another and the withholding of what is due to another.

Illicit sexual expression. Fornication, adultery, and all forms of sexual expression that lack care and concern increase the small-self and hurt people.

Overindulgence in food and drink. Eating and drinking to excess hurts individuals and those whom they contact. Gluttony also contributes to an unjust distribution of the world's resources.

These are the broad categories of behavior that are considered wrong. The wisdom of the ages indicates that to engage in them brings harm to self and/or community. Indeed, to indulge frequently in any of these behaviors leads to the deterioration of human character.

"Do not do to others what you would not like them to do to you" is the classical summary of this minimal standard of morality. If all people could at least hold to this, the world would be a much better place. Just think: no wars, no drunk-driving accidents, no thievery, no pornography! All parents would accept such a world for their children in a split second!

If you find it relatively easy to avoid these major moral pitfalls most of the time, your questions concerning morality have more to do with positive orientations for behavior. If you succeed in avoiding wrong, then what behavior is expected in addition?

In response to this question, the world's religions also seem to be in accord. Their liberating message states that *so long as you are not doing wrong, you may generally do as you wish.* There is much life to be experienced apart from killing, stealing, lying, fornicating, and getting drunk; and — in accord with such thinking — almost anything goes for those who avoid such wrongdoing. The problem, however, which Gotama Buddha pointed up in his teachings on right lifestyle, is that so very much of what is done is indirectly connected with making war, fermenting beverages, and so forth.

For the Christian, right action is to assume an even stronger positive orientation. When the rich young man approached Christ (see Mark 10:17-22), asking about the good life, Jesus quoted to him the minimal moral standards that have been discussed here. When the young man replied that he was keeping these laws, Jesus then encouraged him to give everything to the poor and follow him. The man went away sad; Jesus was asking too much. Elsewhere in the Gospels (see Matthew

25:31-46), Jesus makes it clear that only staying out of trouble is not enough. Because this is a broken, unjust world, the followers of Christ are also called upon to extend God's healing and reconciliation to those in need.

Through the millennia, Catholic Christianity has formulated lists of right actions that enumerate positive means to extend love to others. These challenging lists are summarized in the corporal and spiritual works of mercy.

1. The Corporal Works of Mercy
- To feed the hungry.
- To give drink to the thirsty.
- To clothe the naked.
- To visit the imprisoned.
- To shelter the homeless.
- To visit the sick.
- To bury the dead.

2. The Spiritual Works of Mercy
- To counsel the doubtful.
- To instruct the ignorant.
- To admonish sinners.
- To comfort the afflicted.
- To forgive offenses.
- To bear wrongs patiently.
- To pray for the living and the dead.

As you read over these lists, you are sure to note that it is much harder to do these actions than it is to avoid killing, or stealing, and so forth. And yet most people — even non-Christians — are strangely attracted by the works of mercy. The quality of consciousness presupposed by these actions is also a built-in attraction.

To summarize: Spiritual growth requires that you avoid doing harm to yourself and others while undertaking actions that help other people. The ancient "thou shall nots" point out wrong actions, while the works of mercy point out positive directions for growth.

Reflection/Discussion/Questions

1. With which of the moral avoidances ("thou shall nots") do you struggle? Write out a three-column list of the harmful behaviors, the times you experience them, and the consequences you bring on yourself and others. Now think about your behavior in terms of the First Step of self-help groups: We admitted we were powerless over (alcohol, sex, overeating, for example), and that our lives had become unmanageable.

   • Do you have full control over your behavior? Think of specific ways in which you experience powerlessness (for example, doing something when you don't want to, breaking promises to others, and so forth).
   • How have these behaviors made your life unmanageable?
   • Admit that you have a problem in controlling these compulsive behaviors. This does not mean that you cannot control them; it means that you now recognize that you cannot control them through your will alone.

   Promise yourself that you will seek help (from a counselor, a support group) to deal with your problem. This is part of what it means to acknowledge that you cannot do it alone.

2. Examine the works of mercy. Pick out one or two that can be practiced more fully in your family situation. How will you do this? Make a specific plan, then envision yourself carrying out this plan in your imagination.

9 | Right Desires

"I want very little, and what I do want I have very little wish for" wrote Saint Francis de Sales. "I have hardly any desires, but if I were to be born again, I should have none at all. We should ask nothing and refuse nothing, but leave ourselves in the arms of divine Providence, without wasting time in any desire, except to will what God wills of us."

This kind of tranquil abandonment to divine Providence lies at the end of the spiritual journey, when you live no longer for self, but for God and in God alone. For those who are still functioning at any of the lower ego states (which includes most of humanity), the great saint's words seem to make little sense. No desires? How can this be? How do you find God's will? How do you know *what* to do?

There are simply no satisfactory responses to these kinds of questions. You might as well try to explain to an infant what it is like to live as an adult.

Suffice it to say here that the desirelessness that marks the end of the journey is not complacency, but a perfect resignation to the will of God in each and every moment of the day. And because God is the greatest treasure of all — the pearl of great price (see Matthew 13:44-46) — those who live fully in God have no need for a greater gift.

But what if you are among those who live in the lower realms of consciousness, experiencing desires and knowing you must do something about them? You have your needs and dreams and goals — all of which conspire to give your lives a felt sense of direction. Some of your desires are noble and benevolent; others are fueled by resentment and shame. Sometimes you want to do works of mercy; other times you just want to have a good time and be free of responsibilities. The only thing certain here is that undisciplined desires will eventually lead to an increase in the small-self. Therefore, spiritual training is in order.

In keeping with what was said about right actions, wrong desires can be described as inclinations toward wrong actions — specifically, violence, stealing, improper speech, illicit sex, and overindulgence in food and drink. Quite obviously, if you didn't *want* to do these things, you probably wouldn't. But anyone who works with substance abusers knows what can happen with people who have problems in these areas. The female alcoholic swears she will never get drunk again, but the desire for drink eventually overcomes her resolve to stop. The wife-beater weeps apologetically, pleading for another chance. Later, when his anger becomes uncontrollable, he will beat his wife again.

In disciplining your wrong desires, you need to practice *renunciation*. This means that you make use of your faculties of thought and imagination to help turn your will away from its attraction to harmful behavior. For an example of how this works, consider the case of a married man who finds himself becoming sexually attracted to a female co-worker (who has also made it known that she is attracted to him). If this situation goes unchecked, it is likely that the two will find ways to see each other on the sly. His imagination has already begun creating delicious scenarios, and his excitement has grown to the point where he can scarcely resist any longer. To remedy this situation he will need to do the following:

- Consider how this affair would affect his relationship with his wife, even if she does not find out about it. *(Consequences to self.)*
- Consider what would happen if his wife found out about it — how she would be hurt, how she would react, and so forth. In imagination, he envisions this and allows himself to feel it. *(Consequences to others.)*
- Remember times in the past when he had a similar attraction for other women and how it eventually passed away. *(Transient nature of small-self.)*
- Remember times in the past when he and his wife were close, and how special a person she is to him. *(Positive values at risk.)*
- Note what has happened to the character of friends and family members who break their commitments to their spouses by engaging in illicit sexual affairs. *(Learning from others' mistakes.)*
- Consider how this would affect his relationship with God. *(Religious implications.)*
- Finally, if all of the above tactics fail, he should speak with the woman about his discomfort and request that they not flirt with each other any longer. He may even need to seek a transfer to another area to remove himself physically from her presence. *(Avoidance of the near occasion of sin.)*

By now you are probably thinking that renunciation is very difficult. It is! But the consequences of neglect are also ominous. This is why renunciation skills should be taught at a very early age. In addition to the common situation described above, you might also consider adolescents struggling with peer pressure to use drugs, executives tempted to embezzle company funds, and other similar cases. Without renunciation skills, you are vulnerable to temptation — and there is already enough of that in this world!

Happily, there is another side to this issue, and it is the cultivation of right desires. Because you have wrong desires, you need to practice renunciation; if, however, you cultivate right desires, you will have fewer temptations and so have less need for renunciation.

Benevolence — one of the mega-virtues mentioned in Chapter Seven — is another name for right desires. It means wishing the best for yourself and others — even those whom you do not particularly like. Benevolence is goodwill toward all, because everyone is a brother or sister on the same journey as you. There are no enemies in the benevolent mind; there is not even duality (I-and-thou, us-and-them, and so forth). Only "we" and "us" and our common welfare constitute the focus of benevolence.

As with renunciation, the cultivation of benevolence makes use of other functions of consciousness. The following "pathways" suggested by Ken Keyes, Jr., in his *Handbook to Higher Consciousness* are excellent. Keyes suggests that you repeat these pathways throughout the day — especially when you begin to move into what has been labeled the small-self.

- Open yourself genuinely to all people by being willing to fully communicate your deepest feelings, since hiding in any degree keeps you stuck in your illusion of separateness from other people.
- Feel with loving compassion the problems of others without getting caught up emotionally in their predicaments that are offering them messages they need for their growth.
- Act freely when you are tuned in, centered, and loving, but if possible avoid acting when you are emotionally upset. Otherwise you deprive yourself of the wisdom that flows from love and expanded consciousness.
- Perceive each person, including yourself, as an awakening being who is here to claim his or her birthright to the higher consciousness planes of unconditional love and oneness.

By simply repeating these messages to yourself in private prayer, while riding about in a car, or when interacting with others, you can help to generate benevolence.

In addition to the above pathways, you might make use of imagination to envision yourself behaving kindly toward others. If, for example, you have behaved selfishly with another, you might try sitting quietly in God's presence for a few moments, then reliving the scene where you acted wrongly. You ask God's forgiveness and resolve to make amends; then you pray that God will help you to see yourself behaving differently. In imagination, you again relive the scene; only this time you avoid the wrong and behave kindly. You feel yourself behaving in this new situation and thank God for another option. This kind of positive imaging is a powerful way to re-program your biocomputer.

In this area of right desires it is good to remember that you are not alone in this work of conversion. God is with you! You can do your part by practicing the renunciation and benevolence disciplines described above, but the ultimate work of conversion is going on at a much deeper level. When you surrender your will to God in prayer, he accepts this gift and does his own quiet work. This surrender of the will to God is very important, for without it you are still acting as though you were God. "Thy will be done" is the stance of the person in serenity. If you offer your will to God, he will place his own desires in your heart.

Reflection/Discussion/Questions

1. Surrender yourself and your will to the care of God in prayer. *Pray:* "God, help me to want to do your will, for in your will is my happiness." Repeat this prayer again and again until you are certain that you mean what you are saying.

2. With regard to which temptations do you need to practice the renunciation skills outlined in this chapter? Submit your most harmful temptation to the renunciation exercises outlined in this chapter. Do this for a week, then move on to another temptation for a week. Continue this process, week-after-week, working with the temptations that bother you most.

3. Recall the four benevolence pathways of Ken Keyes, Jr. Repeat them to yourself at least three times a day.

4. Read a Gospel passage in which Jesus is extending benevolence. In imagination, see and feel yourself doing what Jesus is doing in that scene. After a while, shift the scene to a similar circumstance in your own life.

10 | Right Use of Feelings

Feelings are the most personal of all the functions of consciousness. When people tell you how they *think* about something, you get to know something about them. But if they tell you how they *feel* about the same issue, you will know much more about them.

The role of feelings in consciousness is to inform the ego of the meaning of the events that take place in life. In general, this sense of meaning is directly related to your needs and whether or not you believe your needs are being met. If you believe your needs are being met, you experience pleasant feelings; if not, you experience unpleasant feelings of different sorts. Despite this obvious relevance of feelings to spirituality, it is amazing how often their role in transforming consciousness is ignored.

Recall, for a moment, how consciousness functions, as outlined in Figure One on page 14. Note that your feelings result from your *perceptions* of external and internal events (including your own behavior), plus your *consideration* about these events. It's not only what happens to you that stimulates your feelings but what you tell yourself about what happens to you. If someone tells you a snake is dangerous and a threat to your children, you are more likely to experience fear of the snake than if that person told you that snakes have just as much right to be on this planet as you have, and that they are generally no threat if left alone.

Your feelings are closer to your ego than the other functions. The reason for this is that the ego is easily attuned to feeling states. Much of the ego's volitional direction and the quality of awareness is related to feelings. What you *want* is that which will increase or lessen certain feelings; what you are *aware of* is that which will help you to understand those feelings. How you feel at any given moment is thus one of your most important concerns — particularly if you are feeling emotional pain.

The ego becomes "magnetically" focused on physical or psychological pain because, as the responsible center of consciousness, it is the ego's role to do something to alleviate the pain. With pain, then, comes a natural egocentricity. When you are in pain, you are more likely to think about yourself than about others. Therefore, pain is a natural launching pad for the movement of the small-self. Without pain, the small-self has no power to motivate.

In the small-self, you attempt to relieve your discontent by meeting your needs in a selfish manner. Because you want relief now, your small-self is more likely to consider short-term relief than long-term consequences. You eat or drink too much to handle your disappointment; you brag to compensate for your shame; you frantically accumulate wealth to safeguard against insecurity; you try to force others into meeting your needs. But soon these small-self responses not only fail to alleviate your pain but actually increase your discontent. If this movement goes unchecked for too long, you come to a Catch-22, where pain leads to selfish behavior, which leads back again to pain, and so forth. This is addiction.

There is a way off this treadmill, but it is not an easy one. In the long run, you need to live in accordance with your beliefs, and not in response to your feelings. This means that the ego will have to become disentangled from its attachment to feeling states, and this detaching does not come easily. It can be done, however, and the following three steps can help make it happen.

1. Accept all your feelings — good and bad. Do not make a personal judgment of yourself because you are feeling a certain way. Feelings themselves are neither bad nor good; it is not right or wrong to feel a certain way. Nor is it appropriate to say that you should or should not feel something. You feel what you feel! The significant questions are: "What will you do with your feelings, and what will you learn from them?"

2. Learn to express your feelings in an appropriate manner. Feelings denote the presence of energy and, as such, they must be expressed. You do so in certain basic ways:

- *By ignoring/repressing them:* You hide your emotions so that no one knows what you are feeling. This can become such a habit that *you* may not even know what you feel, or that you are repressing. If it happens too much, the energy backs up causing angry outbursts, ulcers, high blood pressure, and general fatigue.
- *By acting them out:* You do what the feeling moves you to do. If angry, you yell and scream; if sad, you cry; if happy, you laugh and grin. This mode of expression releases the energy, and this is good. But you must also consider how this affects others. Violence, for example, is generally an inappropriate way to express anger.
- *By reproaching others:* You blame, criticize, and judge others, making them responsible for your feelings ("You make me so mad!"). This is always inappropriate, for it causes more problems than it solves. Unfortunately, it is also a very common form of emotional expression.
- *By acknowledging them:* "I feel *(good)* about *(this issue)* because *(of these consequences)*," or "I feel *(bad)* when *(this happens)*." This is the best way to communicate feelings to others. In doing so, you own your feelings and describe the circumstances to which they are related.

The manner in which you express your feelings either unites you closer to others (Christ-self), or separates you from others (small-self). It seems to be a fact that most relationship problems result from the inappropriate communication of feelings. When two small-selves start battering each other with "You-messages," intimacy will be destroyed. But when you ask yourself what is the most loving way to express this feeling, you are on a sound pathway to serenity.

3. Learn from your feelings. Recall that your feelings are telling you about how your perceived needs are being met.

- Pleasant, happy feelings result from meeting your wants and needs.
- Disappointment results from not getting what you expected.
- Anger results from disappointment and hurt.
- Fear results from perceiving a problem that threatens the fulfillment of your wants/needs as having no solution.
- Guilt results from doing something contrary to your values.
- Arrogance results from thinking you are better than others.
- Sadness results from losing an important person, place, or thing or even part of yourself.

This point should now be clear. If, for example, you feel disappointment, then you must accept the feeling (Step 1), express it appropriately (Step 2), and then learn from it (Step 3). If you do not take Steps 1 and 2, you will not be able to learn anything, for your disappointment will keep cycling round and round in a stimulus-response loop, and you will not change. After taking Steps 1 and 2, you can begin asking yourself such questions as, "Why am I disappointed? What was I expecting? Was this expectation legitimate? Do I need to change my expectations so they will be more reasonable?"

This last question points up the value of simplicity. If you want lots of things and you have many set hopes, you will experience a great deal of disappointment, anger, and fear. If, on the other hand, you desire less, you will less frequently meet with frustration. According to the Buddhists (who have much to teach us about pain), emotional pain is the gap between a want and its fulfillment. Those who want nothing — we are back to desirelessness — will therefore experience no emotional pain. The great religious leaders and saints of the ages were usually simple and uncomplicated people. The Buddha died in poverty, and the Son of Man had no place to lay his head.

In regard to the ego then, it can be seen that the reduction of emotional pain in your life should free the ego to care for other concerns. This reduction comes from living less in the small-self, by practicing the three steps outlined above, and by making use of the other living skills described in this section. As you begin to resolve your painful issues more out of love, you will experience less emotional suffering. In time, after you have dealt with your painful Shadows, even the ego itself will disappear. What will be left in its place is the Cosmic Christ-self, which lives more by grace and reason than by feeling. No longer then will feelings be responsive to "me," "my," and "mine," but to "we," "us," and "ours." It was in this manner that Christ wept over Jerusalem while never complaining about his own pain.

Reflection/Discussion/Questions

1. What kinds of feelings do you experience most frequently in your life? Rank these feelings in terms of most frequent to the least.

2. How do you generally express your own feelings? Consider the four modes of expression discussed in this chapter.

3. Do you accept yourself and your feelings without judgment? Explain.

4. What do you learn about yourself from your different feelings? What lessons are they teaching you about your wants/needs? Your self-image? Your religious values?

5. For the next two weeks, take a few moments at the end of each day to learn from your feelings. You may want to line them up in the following manner:
- What did you feel?
- What were the circumstances?
- How did you express your feelings?
- What do these feelings teach you about your wants, expectations, and values?

11 | Right Beliefs

"As a man thinketh, so he is," reads an old adage. The truth of this saying is evident in many places throughout this book. For example, if you think you are stupid, you will feel and behave as though you are. If you believe a snake is dangerous, you will react to it differently than if you think it is friendly. Thinking is the pivotal factor in the development of conduct, character, and consciousness — the "three c's" of the spiritual life.

From whence come your thoughts, however? If you knew the complete answer to this question, you would have a much better understanding of the metaphysical nature of a human being. Surely your thoughts derive from a number of sources. With regard to spiritual growth, however, it seems that most of your thoughts derive from your *beliefs* about God, human nature, and the meaning of life in general.

There is, then, a definite connection between thoughts and beliefs. Many philosophers define thoughts as the symbolic constructs of the intellect *by means of which* persons comprehend the nature of reality. In contrast to feelings, which are concerned with personal meaning, thinking is concerned with the truth of a situation. If, during the course of time, you repeatedly think about something in a certain manner, it will become a belief. When this pattern of thinking becomes a belief, it in turn influences the thoughts you have about the subject in question. *Beliefs might thus be considered as specific thought patterns that have been committed to memory.*

In a very real way, you don't have your beliefs; they have you. Without even being conscious of it, everything that happens to you is filtered through your belief system. Your perceptions are like light entering a prism; your beliefs are the prism that "filters" the light rays, bending them this way and that; your thoughts are the energies that emerge from the prism; your feelings are the warmth or coldness of the energies. By listening to your thoughts and feelings, then, you can trace them to their origin in your beliefs. As long as you hold unhealthy beliefs, however, you will remain powerless over the kinds of thoughts and feelings which they produce.

For a practical example of how this works, suppose you are a man who is feeling angry (and thus hurt and disappointed) because a woman colleague got a promotion at work for which you had also applied. If you go through the three-step process for dealing with feelings described in Chapter 10, you will come to a place where you ask yourself, "Why am I disappointed? Which expectations of mine were not met?" You may discover that, for a number of reasons, you really wanted this promotion because it meant higher pay, more interesting work, a change from the present "rut," and other benefits. This accounts for some of your anger, but the fact that a *woman* got the job and not you is also a part of your disappointment. In deep, prayerful silence, you trace your thoughts about women in the workplace back to their roots in beliefs, where, finally, you hear your thoughts repeating in dogmatic fashion the following statements:

"Women belong in the home, not in the workplace."

"When another person is chosen before you, it means you are a loser."

"To lose to a woman is a disgrace."

At this point, you may choose to reaffirm your beliefs and thus persist in your feelings of anger and jealousy, or you may decide to challenge these beliefs and re-program them. (The fact that such re-programming is possible should be one of the most exciting discoveries in life!) You might counter your old beliefs as follows:

"Women have just as much a right to work as I have."

"It does not mean I am inferior when another person is chosen before me."

"It is no disgrace to lose out to a woman; in fact, this woman is superbly qualified for the promotion."

"Besides, there's nothing I can do to change the boss' mind."

Meditating on these thoughts will fix them in your prism of beliefs. Your emotional response to your colleague's promotion will become less negative; your own serenity will deepen.

It should be noted here that beliefs come from many sources. As the man in the above example, your particular beliefs no doubt come from your home, your Church, and your childhood friends. Note, too, that these are all value-oriented beliefs rather than scientific beliefs, which can be validated through experimentation. There are many beliefs in your filtering prisms, and they were all programmed through different sources. Some are based on ignorance and can be corrected with knowledge; others may be based on prejudice and can be corrected through benevolence.

The kinds of beliefs treated in this book have to do with God, human nature, and the meaning of life. Your beliefs in these areas are rooted in the deepest parts of your intellectual filtering prism. They are also among the most dogmatic of all beliefs, as evidenced by the rigidity of thoughts and intensity of feelings that they generate. The reason for this is because such religious beliefs are some of the most significant ways in which you define yourself as a human being.

To change your belief about God or human nature or life's meaning is difficult because it means that you, too, must change your basic manner of being human. This kind of change is generally resisted by the ego, for the ego is a basically conservative psychic structure. However, growth through the years brings the realization that real life is larger than earlier religious beliefs can accommodate. When this happens you must either go through the pain and insecurity that accompany the reworking of religious beliefs or else succumb to the dogmatism of old beliefs and die. The first option is a choice for the living God; the second is idolatry.

In discussing right beliefs about God, human nature, and the meaning of life, you may ask what it is that makes beliefs right or wrong. "Aren't religious beliefs a purely subjective matter?"

Religious beliefs are indeed personal, subjective matters. As with right actions and desires previously discussed, right beliefs are those that help to diminish the small self and increase the Christ-self. Right beliefs may also be understood as those which help to produce right desires, right decisions, and right behaviors. But it is obvious that all this talk of right and wrong is of a different domain than the objectivity of scientific truth. Instead, it is based here upon the world view of Christianity — a view which overlaps considerably with many other world religions.

What follows here will be short, simple dogmatic statements about God, human nature, and the meaning of life. The reason for this is that beliefs are precisely such dogmatic and essential statements; everything else is embellishment and sophisticated refinement of the essential beliefs. Most homilies and spiritual books manage to influence these outer layers of embellishment; they seldom result in changing essential beliefs. This will not be an attempt to present a list of the *only* essential beliefs in Christianity. The beliefs listed below were compiled with a view toward facilitating the right desires and right actions discussed in previous chapters and not to enumerate a comprehensive listing of all essential Christian beliefs.

It is also important to consider the relation of beliefs to one another. None of the beliefs listed below should be taken out of context from the rest. They all say something unique, but they also modify and support each other. For example, most religions acknowledge a Creator God; a few state that this Creator is loving; fewer yet state that this loving Creator wants to be in relationship with people; only one states that Jesus Christ is God come to establish that loving relationship. Keeping these considerations about essential beliefs in mind, here is a list covering the three areas mentioned in this chapter:

1. Right Beliefs About God

- God is Spirit.
- God is Love.
- God is immanent and transcendent.
- God is Creator of all that is.
- God wants to be in relationship with humanity.
- Jesus Christ is God incarnate.
- God can forgive all wrongdoing.
- The Holy Spirit joins people with Christ and the Father.
- People's conceptions of God are always inadequate.

2. Right Beliefs About Human Nature

- People are a holistic blend of body, mind, and spirit.
- God is the ground of all humanity. All people are children of God.
- The functions of consciousness are the property of the person and can be changed by a person.
- The functions of consciousness have been distorted by sin which causes them to center readily on fear and selfishness.
- The functions of consciousness can be energized by God if God is invited to do so.

3. Right Beliefs About Life's Meaning

- Life is a very special gift that is to be accepted in gratitude.
- Life is short, and it will end in death.
- Life gives all people the opportunity to define the kind of persons they wish to be.

- Eternal destiny is determined by the decisions made in this life.
- Selfishness brings isolation and misery; love brings happiness and unity.
- The way to eternal life in God comes from living in the truth and love of Christ.
- All must work hard, using their talents for good.
- The good and simple pleasures of life are to be enjoyed in gratitude.
- Suffering is a part of this life, but it teaches many valuable lessons.

If you meditate upon these simple belief statements, you will shape your belief prism in such a manner as to transform your feelings, desires, decisions, and behavior in accordance with the energies of the Christ-self. You will come to live as God intended you to live. You will live in the reign of God, and you will be truly happy.

Reflection/Discussion/Questions

1. What have you learned about your beliefs from your meditation on the preceding chapters? How do beliefs affect your feelings, desires, and behavior? Which beliefs do you wish to change?

2. With which of the beliefs presented in this chapter do you agree? Disagree? Why?

3. How do you respond to others who do not believe as you do? What does this teach you about your own beliefs?

4. Read the Gospels each day and meditate on their message to help implant healthy beliefs into your mind.

5. Ask a priest or minister to recommend spiritual reading material to help shape your beliefs about God, human nature, and the meaning of life. (The Suggested Reading list in this book also provides a list of helpful reading material.)

12 Right Values

As with the beliefs described in Chapter Eleven, values are thoughts which have been committed to memory. Values are beliefs, but unlike the theological and philosophical kinds presented in Chapter Eleven, they are concerned with the manner in which you meet your basic wants/needs. Values assume a very practical orientation; they ask what? when? how much? how? and other pertinent questions.

You begin learning values early in life. The passionate, undisciplined energy of the child is disciplined by the parents so that, by the age of six, an internal Parent state (superego) has developed to provide internal guidance for behavior. Values during this period are largely understood as do/don't, should/shouldn't, yes/no. The reasoning behind the value may be known and appreciated, but the power of the value to discipline behavior arises from its source in parental approval and disapproval. The real meaning of this Parent state may be unhealthy or healthy, depending on how these values are communicated. Some persons suffer from very rigid, judgmental, and shaming superegos, while others are sociopaths who seem to have almost no internal ego-Parent strictures.

As you grow through the years, you add new dimensions to your values. The adolescent will generally adopt some of the values of the peer group (Persona state). If these values are in conflict with the Parent state — as well as flesh-and-blood parents — a turbulent civil war will be waged internally and externally in heated discussions with parents. This civil war is slightly diminished when, in the late teens and early twenties, you move into the Conscientious state and begin to make these values your own. It is the major task of adolescence to translate values from the Parent state through the Persona state to the Conscientious state.

As an example of how this works, consider the following case. John was accustomed to visiting his grandparents through the years. When he was a child he enjoyed spending time with them and he spent the night or the weekend with them whenever possible. As he got older, however, he preferred to spend this time with his friends; consequently, his relationship with his grandparents lessened quite a bit. Then the time came when they could no longer care for themselves, so they went to a nursing home. During John's weekend visits from college, his father — in typical Parent manner — would remind him that his grandparents might not be around much longer, and he'd best visit every chance he could. A young man in graduate school is not likely to appreciate Parent state messages any longer, and John was no exception (especially since the message came from the source itself). Nevertheless, he went to visit his grandparents at the nursing home, but largely to avoid guilt. Upon returning to college after one such visitation, he asked himself if he really did love his grandparents, and if he really did want a relationship with them. Quite happily, the answer to both questions was "yes"! He then began to visit his grandparents out of choice, not out of obligation. A superego value had been translated into a Conscientious state value.

As your personal growth unfolds beyond the Conscientious state, values generally change very little. A successful confrontation with the Shadow state usually results in a final break with the last of your superego ties. But by the time you begin living in the Adult state, it is no longer a question of choosing the values by which you shall live; this is the task of the Conscientious state. The task of the Adult state is to *live* by these values. In the Adult state, character development is an ongoing struggle to become the person implicit in your values. You incarnate what you believe. Finally, in the Cosmic state, you have *become* your values. Who you are and what you believe are one and the same, although growth continues. The internal civil war that began during childhood and intensified during adolescence is finally resolved in the Cosmic state.

Given such a complicated developmental process, it should be obvious that any attempt to speak of right values will surely be difficult. But the basic question must be asked: What is a right value and what makes it right?

Right values may be described as *forces which lead to right desires and right behaviors*. Ultimately, right values consist of those beliefs that enable you to meet your basic wants/needs in such a manner as to harm no one and to build up the human community. For Christians, these values are further focused by reflecting on the teachings of Christ and the Church.

As for the different approaches to values found in the various ego states, very little can be done to simplify this issue. But here is a brief sketch which shows the kinds of beliefs and practices that can help you to grow in these different values. Whether you undertake this project out of obligation (Parent state), peer pressure (Persona state), or because of its ideological appeal (Conscientious state) does not change the focus of the values as guidelines for meeting needs. Most likely, your beginning motives make very little difference here anyway. You begin where you are and you grow as the Lord leads you. What is important is that you undertake the struggle to incorporate healthy values into your biocomputer, and then to live by them as fully as possible.

There are five major values you should strive to cultivate:

temperance, humility, prudence, justice, and fortitude. Those who are familiar with traditional morality will recognize here the old cardinal virtues (with the addition of humility). But it should be remembered that even these five values are secondary to the three mega-values of awareness, honesty, and benevolence (which, on a spiritual plane, correspond to faith, hope, and charity). The cardinal virtues (plus humility) are really the means by which you demonstrate God's love in the concrete circumstances of your life. Listed below are those values and suggestions for making them your own.

Temperance is defined as the practice of moderation to meet your bodily needs in an appropriate manner.

1. Beliefs

- You are stewards of your bodies. It is your responsibility to properly care for your bodies.
- The human body is good. It is a temple of the Holy Spirit. As you treat your bodies, so do you treat the Lord.
- In the area of sexuality, you recognize that sex is not merely a physical act; it also involves emotional and spiritual bonding. Therefore, you regard your sexuality as a gift to be shared fully only with those who pledge love and faithfulness.

2. Practices

- Study to learn about the body's nutritional needs.
- Commit yourself to a balanced, nutritional diet.
- Take proper exercise. Give your heart a good workout for 15-20 minutes at least three times a week. Also, keep your muscles in tone.
- Get proper rest. Adults need about seven hours of sleep each night. Children can use eight or nine.
- Don't use illegal drugs. If you drink, do it responsibly. Learn your limits; don't get high. Don't smoke cigarettes; quit if you have already started.
- Avoid indulging in sexual fantasies. You can't help having

thoughts about sex, but you can avoid giving in to them. Avoidance might mean something as simple as refusing to look at pornographic magazines.

- Learn to recognize your stress signals. A churning stomach, nail biting, and clenching fists all indicate a need to slow down, take a few deep breaths, and unwind.

Humility means being honest about your strengths and weaknesses as you strive to meet your esteem needs.

1. Beliefs

- No one is perfect; this includes you.
- No one is completely bad; this includes you.
- God loves you and he wants you to love him in return.
- You are a unique individual — a combination of forces that has never before existed and will never exist again.

2. Practices

- Accept your thoughts, feelings, and desires without putting yourself down.
- Acknowledge your giftedness in gratitude.
- Acknowledge your limitations without shame.
- Acknowledge your selfishness with remorse.
- Acknowledge your need for God.

Prudence is the wise and practical approach to the fulfillment of your needs — material, relational, psychic, and so forth.

1. Beliefs

- It is a good thing to do as much for yourself as possible. If others do for you what you should do for yourself, you become dependent upon them.
- It is a good thing to allow others to do for you what you cannot do for yourself. If you refuse their help, you become proud and lonely.

- It is important to distinguish between wants and needs. Keep it simple. Needs are those things which, if neglected, lead to death; wants are the rest.
- God is a providential God, leading you to people and circumstances that will enable you to grow and prosper. You shall always have what you need when you truly need it.

2. Practices

- Define your needs/wants as simply as possible and desire no more than this. Practice renunciation in situations characterized by excess.
- Identify resources necessary to the securing of your needs.
- Make a budget, listing expenses to meet your needs/wants and sources of income to secure these goods.
- Do honest work to secure your needs.
- Ask for help when you see you can't do the work alone.
- Pray for your specific needs, knowing that God is generous.

Justice consists in giving all people their due. It is service that furthers human rights. Such service is basic to Christianity.

1. Beliefs

- The world in general treats people unfairly.
- Some people are born into very difficult circumstances; others are more fortunate.
- Those who have much are responsible for using their gifts to help those who have little.
- Impressing other people is a very shallow way to attain status. What if they change their minds?
- Christ works with you to restore the world. You restore it with Christ.
- Ministry to your brothers and sisters is ministry to Christ.

- Status attained through service will never exceed your integrity; status artificially bestowed will rob you of integrity.

2. Practices

- Meditate on the spiritual and corporal works of mercy.
- Identify specific circumstances in your life to which you are called in order to practice works of mercy.
- Avoid temptations to impress other people with your lifestyle and your works by practicing right desires and right speech.

Fortitude is described as courage or strength of character that enables you to be assertive for good.

1. Beliefs

- Your free will helps you to avoid evil and do good. Your greatest freedom is to use your will for good.
- You recognize that other people also have free will, and that your freedom cannot be exercised at the expense of their welfare.

2. Practices

- Never do for others what they can and should do for themselves.
- Allow others the freedom to make their mistakes and to learn from them.
- Meditate on the fact that all things are possible when you act in union with God.
- Counter your fearfulness by asserting yourself in behalf of goodness.
- After doing what you can, wait patiently on the Lord for results.

Lengthy books have been written about each of these values. This listing of core beliefs and practices is only intended to focus consciousness in the right direction. It is intended to lead you to further reading and study in this area.

Ideally, the living out of Christian values takes place in a community of believers. It is in community that you ask for feedback concerning needs and wants, justice issues, and other matters. In the absence of such a community of dialogue, discernment with regard to values is a very difficult task. It would be wonderful indeed if all Christians were deeply involved in support groups committed to seriously living out Christian values! Such a development would surely be a step in the direction toward global peace.

Reflection/Discussion/Questions

1. With which of the values listed in this chapter do you struggle most? What needs to happen for you in this area?

2. How do you experience your values? From a Parent state? From a Persona state? From a Conscientious state? Examine Figure Four on page 36 for your response.

3. How have your values changed through the years? Choose one of the values discussed in this chapter and trace its development through the years.

4. What would you like to learn about values from other Christians? If you are in a support group, ask for feedback.

13 | Right Awareness

An old Eastern story recounts the words of a Zen master who celebrated his enlightenment with the following words: "Oh wondrous marvel: I chop wood! I draw water from the well!"

This story does not sound very exciting; but once its meaning is apprehended it becomes provocative indeed.

Upon attaining enlightenment, the Zen master experienced a unification of body, mind, and spirit. Consequently, he became totally present to whatever he was doing, whether it was chopping wood or drawing water from the well. When he says, "I chop wood," he means that this is *all* that he does. He does not mull over yesterday's fight with his wife or the declining prices of stocks or his vacation coming up next week. He simply chops wood, and it is enough. He is NOW/HERE, rather than NO/WHERE, which is the state of the divided mind.

The Buddhists have perhaps made the greatest contribution among the world religions in pointing out the importance of right awareness (called Right Mindfulness and Right Concentration in the Eightfold Path). Some Buddhist teachers distinguish three kinds of awareness. *Negative* awareness exists when you are preoccupied with various thoughts and concerns to the extent that you are not fully present to the moment. *Personal* awareness exists when you are present to the moment in an I-Thou manner; you are the observer in the present moment. *Absolute* awareness exists when even this sense of I-Thou has been lost because you have become unitively joined with creation; it is completely subjective awareness. Few people in this world come to live completely in the state of absolute awareness (which in this book is called Cosmic Consciousness); but, like most people, you can experience this for short periods of time. You can also train your awareness so that you spend less time in negative awareness and more time in personal awareness.

As with Buddha and other spiritual geniuses, Jesus places a high value on acute awareness. Time and again, he stresses the importance of staying awake (see Mark 13:33). In the Garden of Gethsemane, he invites his apostles to "remain here and keep watch with me" (Matthew 26:38). When they fall asleep he expresses great disappointment. For Jesus, it is the unaware mind that is the devil's playground. "Be sure of this:" he says, "if the master of the house had known the hour of night when the thief was coming, he would have stayed awake and not let his house be broken into" (Matthew 24:43). If you are not at home in your house (that is, consciousness), then you are vulnerable to all sorts of negative energies.

Everything that has ever happened to you has happened in a now-moment, and everything that will happen to you in the future will happen in a now-moment. Why, then, do so many live in the NO/WHERE of negative awareness?

The teachings of both Eastern and Western mystics can help you in your struggle with this issue. You will learn from them that there are three reasons for your failure to live as fully as you should in the NOW.

1. Unreconciled guilt, shame, and resentment in connection with past experiences. (Emotional pain.)
2. Worries and fixed hopes in connection with the future. (More emotional pain.)
3. Lack of now-moment discipline with regard to the present.

Each of these problems will be treated separately, although they all have in common the manner in which they are faced in time.

Reconciling With the Past

It has been said that when you remember your past, you are re-membered, or made one with your past. Such remembering is very healthy. This is why the Lord asked to be remembered in "the breaking of the bread." If you do not take time to remember, you forget who you were and, consequently, who you are at the present moment. That much-quoted line of Santayana's also rings true here: "Those who forget the past are doomed to repeat it." In truth, you learn nothing from experience; you learn only by *reflecting* on your experiences.

While remembering is healthy, *clinging* to the past is another matter altogether. You cling to the past when you keep reliving situations over and over again. You play "if only" games, each time making yourself look better than the reality itself. The reason you cling is usually because the past holds unreconciled pains such as guilt, shame, and resentment. As long as there is unreconciled pain in the past, the ego will spontaneously direct its gaze in that direction. What is needed in such cases is a healing of memories.

Perhaps the best process for healing memories can be found in Steps 4, 5, 8, and 9 of Alcoholics Anonymous. In these Steps, you are asked to do the following:

- Make a searching and fearless moral inventory of yourself.
- Admit to God, to yourself, and to another human being the exact nature of your wrongs.

- Make a list of persons you have harmed, and be willing to make amends to them.
- Make direct amends to such people wherever possible, except when to do so would injure them or others.

These four Steps help you to own up to your own part in past hurts, and it is essential that you do so. If you do not take these Steps, it will be very difficult to forgive and accept yourself.

But what about hurts that others have inflicted? The answer again is to be found in forgiveness. You are to forgive others all the wrongs they have done, however malicious they may have been. The reason you do this is not to excuse their behavior, nor even less to pretend it never happened. You forgive in order to let go of resentments. As long as you resent others, you are clinging to the past, and you are not free. It is of utmost importance that you become *willing* to forgive others the wrongs they have done. If forgiveness of this kind seems difficult, then this is all the more reason to pray for it and to ask others to pray for you too. Many times forgiveness comes slowly; other times, it is given in a moment, like a breath of fresh air. Generally, it is also necessary that you find some type of group in which to express hurtful feelings in the manner described in Chapter Ten.

Having forgiven others and expressed your pain, it is also important that you learn what you can from your past hurts. What happened? Why did it happen? What role did you play? What needs to be affirmed? What will you do differently next time? It is by reflecting upon questions like these that you learn not to repeat experiences that proved painful in the past. Such reflection and forgiveness frees the ego from its clinging attachment to the past so that you can live more fully in the present and provide more responsibly for the future.

Facing the Future

Because you live in time as a conscious being, it is possible not only to remember the past and experience the present but also to anticipate the future. It is impossible for a healthy human being to ignore the future. The problem arises when you view the future with anxiety, concern, and fixed expectations.

Breaking free from past hurts will generally do much to heal unnecessary concerns for the future, for many of your worries derive from projecting past hurts. If, for example, you have been rejected in a romantic relationship, it will be natural to project this hurt into the future as a fear of rejection. When this hurt has become healed through forgiveness, and when you learn the lessons implicit in this experience through reflection, you strip the projecting mechanism of much of its paranoid energy.

The very best way to face the future is in hopeful trust. No matter what the past has been, you trust that your providential God has something better in mind for you. Maintaining such an open, hopeful attitude is very difficult, for the general tendency is to formulate fixed expectations concerning how you would like God to take care of you. These fixed expectations make for a fearful clinging to the future — another great enemy of serenity.

Now this does not mean that you should do away with goals, objectives, and expectations in general. Formulating an intelligent plan to face the future is part of the virtue of prudence. By fixed expectations is meant that you require things to turn out the way you want, or else you will be disappointed. The content of these expectations can be anything — career advancement, the economy, the success of your favorite football team, your children's choices of careers, and so forth. When you formulate fixed expectations, you make yourself vulnerable to disappointment. As long as such vulnerability exists, there will dwell alongside it the *fear* of disappointment.

What is to be done, then? How are you to face the future without setting yourself up for disappointment?

In response to these questions, you might try the following:

- Practice the virtue of prudence with regard to providing for your needs (see pages 77-78).
- Make your plans, but be willing to change your mind. Maybe God has something better in mind for you.

- Pray the Serenity Prayer: "God, grant me the serenity to accept the things I cannot change, courage to change the things I can, and the wisdom to know the difference." Ask yourself what you can control and what you are unable to control. Allow God to take care of what you cannot control.
- Renounce such attitudes as, "I'll be OK when . . . " and similar sentiments. The future is merely another present moment just like this one. If you can't find contentment now, you won't find it in the future.
- Meditate on the transience of all life and the inevitability of death. Unless you face the fact of your mortality, you give power to the fear of death. The truth is that serenity does not come from cheating death, but from accepting death as a transition to a new, spiritual existence.

Many times in the Gospels Jesus tells his followers to let go of anxiety. "God is with you now" is his message. If you can learn to live in this awareness in the present, you become free to face the future in trust, for the God who is with you now shall be with you in that forthcoming present moment that is called the future.

Living in the Present

Making peace with the past and the future enables you to live more fully in the present moment. Nevertheless, this possibility will not be experienced without cultivating a certain amount of discipline.

A first problem that you encounter concerns the focus of attention itself. If you do not focus on past or future, then what exactly do you pay attention to? After all, there are so many things going on around you in this moment that it is sometimes difficult to decide just which way you ought to turn your gaze.

Actually, the question of where to direct your attention is a matter of discernment, which will be taken up in the next chapter. The main lesson here is that whatever you decide to do with your attention, *you should be there with it*. You strive as much as possible to avoid the fragmentation of negative awareness by paying attention to what you are doing. If you are chopping wood, you chop wood; if you decide to drink water, you drink water; if you are planning a future event or remembering a past experience, then you do those things in awareness. "Do what you are doing" is a slogan that is most helpful in cultivating present-moment awareness.

To cultivate right awareness, it is not necessary to do a lot of willful concentrating. Actually, the opposite is true: The most important discipline for living in the now is not willfulness, but surrender. The more willful you are, the less likely it is that you will experience the realities of this moment; the more you let go into the now, the more fully you experience present reality. When you surrender to the now, you relax, let your guard down, and allow reality to simply flow through you (sort of like when you are watching a good movie). When you are willful, you tense up and approach reality in an attitude of imperialistic domination. Willfulness has you reacting to the environment; surrendering permits you to respond. The discovery of this dynamic of surrender will be one of the happiest paradoxes you will encounter on your spiritual journey.

Several disciplines that will enable you to grow in your experience of surrendering to the moment are listed here:

- Take a few minutes each day to be present to creation. Simply look, listen, smell, feel. If you start to have thoughts about it, don't indulge them. Keep gazing and allow creation to enter into you so that you become one with the objects of your attention.
- Learn to separate your awareness from your thoughts and feelings. Remember, you are not your thoughts and feelings. Say to yourself: "I am thinking this, I am feeling that." Do not judge yourself for these thoughts and feelings.
- Make a list of all that needs to be done during the day so that your mind does not keep going over it repeatedly. Decide what needs to be done first, then second, and so on.
- Surrender yourself fully to what you are doing. Be there with your senses, your thoughts, your feelings.

- Become more open to experiencing yourself as a bodily person. Your body is always in the now; get in touch with its sensations and needs. Disciplines such as yoga, relaxation exercises, biofeedback, and focusing can help you to live more fully in the present.
- Take quiet time to place yourself in the presence of God. Imagine that the atmosphere is an ocean of God, and you are inhaling and exhaling God. After a while, you become so joined with God as to be one with him. If any thoughts creep in, do not indulge them; simply return to your breathing in God's presence.

This last point in particular is most helpful, for it calms the restless, scanning mind more than anything else. Apparently, acute awareness is open to both empirical and spiritual reality. It is difficult to stay focused in either one without also attending the other. By allowing your awareness to rest in God's awareness of you (which is the fruit of contemplative prayer), you thus open yourself to the splendid awareness of creation as a manifestation of God. When your attention is fully grounded in spiritual and empirical reality, living in the present moment is a heavenly experience.

Reflection/Discussion/Questions

1. In which kind of awareness do you spend most of your time: negative, personal, or absolute?

2. Take time to do Steps 4, 5, 8, and 9 of AA. If you need guidance, ask a member of this fellowship, or purchase a copy of *Becoming a New Person: Twelve Steps to Christian Growth*.

3. How do you view the future? Are there set expectations you need to let go of?

4. Make a commitment to take quiet time in order to practice the awareness exercises described in this chapter.

14 | Right Discernment

One of the peculiar characteristics of human nature is that you spend much of your time being other than what you really are. Birds know how to be birds, and snakes always act according to their true nature. Not even plants can be accused of phoniness; they are simply themselves. Yet, according to the world's great religions, you as human beings are children of God. In a Christian context, this means that you are, in your deepest nature, beings of Love. To realize this is to also acknowledge that you often behave in a very unloving manner.

Supposedly, all animals have to make decisions, although certainly they do not do so in a very great awareness. But it is very likely that a bird, for example, must decide whether it will fly away from a branch or stay there. Whatever its decision, the bird will have lost none of its bird-ness as a consequence of its decision. This is not the case with human beings, however.

Without launching into an exhaustive reflection on the nature of fallen humanity, it will be helpful here to point out that what most people call human nature is nothing but the egocentric, small-self. In this self, reality is viewed in terms of narrow self-interest, and decisions are made accordingly. In contrast to this, the Christ-self involves a love relationship with God, others, and creation. When you make decisions that increase your selfishness, you come away a little less human than if you had acted in love.

So you see that the kinds of decisions you make bring consequences not only in areas of behavior but also in terms of identity as well. When you make a selfish choice, you not only hurt yourself and others because of your selfish behavior but you also become a more selfish — hence, less human — person.

In terms of the functions of consciousness, decision-making is the will acting on perceptions, beliefs, and feelings. *Decision-making can thus be viewed as the primary activity in which you define yourself as a human being*. Decisions are the touchstones of incarnation; as you act, so you become, and as you become, so you act.

The references to right discernment made in this chapter refer to the processes by which you make decisions. More specifically, discernment has its focus in God's will and in the choice of God's preference for you among a number of options. The reason why you engage in a process of discernment is because you believe that it is by doing God's will that you find serenity, and thus become the person God created you to be.

It is obvious that many people do not undertake a process of discernment in making important decisions. In the small-self, there is no question of checking out your decisions with God; you simply do what you want. But many people of goodwill — even committed Christians — bypass the step of discernment for a number of reasons. Some were never taught the principles of discernment outlined in this chapter. Others look upon discernment as a sign of scrupulosity, and so naïvely assume that whatever they decide is God's will for them. The most common obstacle to discernment, however, is a lack of faith. If you do not really believe that God's will is your happiness, then it follows that you will look upon discernment with little enthusiasm. It is quite another matter to believe in a good and providential God who is leading you in the optimal unfolding of your personhood.

Discernment, then, is based on the following assumptions:

- God is a good God. He wants to give you much more than you want for yourself.
- God knows who you are better than you know yourself. God also knows what you need in order to become the person he created you to be better than you know what you need for this.
- When you are faced with a number of options, it is entirely possible that some of these options are better for you in terms of your overall human objectives than others.
- When you surrender your preferences for different options to God, you become free to discern God's preference (if any) among these options.

Unless you accept these assumptions (at least on an intellectual level), the guidelines that follow will not make much sense.

The truly great master of the art of discernment was Saint Ignatius of Loyola. His writings on making choices and discerning God's call have stood the test of time and continue to provide a helpful structure for choosing among options. For this reason the guidelines presented here rely heavily upon the genius of Ignatius.

1. "When you are making a decision or choice, you are not deliberating about choices which involve sin [wrongdoing], but rather you are considering alternatives which are lawful and good . . . " (Saint Ignatius).

2. It is not necessary to agonize over God's will in choosing between healthy options in the small affairs of everyday life. "Ordinarily there is nothing of such obvious importance in one rather than the other that there is need to go into long deliberation over it. You must proceed in good faith and

without making subtle distinctions in such affairs and, as Saint Basil says, do freely what seems good to you, so as not to weary your mind, waste your time, and put yourself in danger of disquiet, scruples, and superstition" (Saint Francis de Sales).

3. In areas where you have binding commitments (marriage vows, parenting, religious vows, and so forth), "your basic attitude should be that the only choice still called for is the full-hearted gift of self to this state of life" (Saint Ignatius). In other words, every effort must be made to live out the implications of your binding commitments, even if those commitments were poorly made.

4. In areas of life where you have already made decisions (which can be changed) on the basis of God's call, "your one desire should be to find your continued growth in the way of life you have chosen" (Saint Ignatius).

5. "If you have come to a poor decision in matters that are changeable, you should try to make a choice in the proper way whether it would be maintaining the same pattern of life or it would demand a change" (Saint Ignatius).

6. If possible, you should avoid making important life decisions during times when you are emotionally upset, for it is likely that you shall then be running away from a problem rather than responding to God's call.

7. When attempting to discern among a number of options regarding significant lifestyle choices, you should proceed as Saint Ignatius suggests in the following patterns.

A. **First Pattern:**
   • Clearly place before your mind what it is you want to decide about. What are your options?
   • Attempt to view each option with equal detachment, surrendering personal preferences to God.

- Sincerely pray that God will enlighten and draw you in the direction leading to his praise and glory.
- List and weigh the advantages and disadvantages of the various dimensions of your proposed decision.
- Consider now which alternative seems more reasonable. Then decide according to the more weighty motives and not from any selfish or sensual inclination.
- Having come to the decision, now turn to God again and ask him to accept and confirm it — if it is for his greater service and glory — by giving you a sense of serenity and holy conviction about this decision.

B. Second Pattern: (This is an excellent follow-up on the First Pattern to "objectively" evaluate your decision.)

- Since the love of God should motivate your life, you should check yourself to see whether your attachment for the object of choice is solely because of your Creator and Lord.
- Imagine yourself in the presence of a person whom you have never met before but who has sought your help in an attempt to respond better to God's call. Review what you would tell that person and then observe the advice which you would so readily give to another for whom you want the best.
- Ask yourself if at the moment of death you would make the same decision you are making now. Guide yourself by this insight and make your present decision in conformity with it.
- See yourself standing before Christ your Judge when this life has ended and talking with him about the decision which you have made at this moment in your life. Choose now the course of action which you feel will give you happiness and joy in the presence of Christ on the Day of Judgment.

There is a big difference between reacting to life and responding to God's call. In the small-self, you spend a lot of time reacting to life; you allow other people and circumstances to greatly influence your behavior. By undertaking a decision-making process such as that outlined above, you become more pro-active, or responsive to God's call. As with all the other spiritual living skills, right discernment will involve practice and checking matters out with the community. The fruit of this discernment will be fuller growth and deeper serenity — two very good reasons to persist in the struggle to discern God's call.

This chapter concludes the treatment of the seven living skills .so necessary for spiritual growth. The following chapter will sum up the preceding by showing the intimate connection between spirituality and grace.

Reflection/Discussion/Questions

1. What kinds of binding commitments have you made? How do you feel about living out these commitments in loving persistence? How has this persistence changed you?

2. What kinds of important, nonbinding decisions have you made? How do you feel about continuing to live out these decisions?

3. What kinds of poor decisions have you made? How have they changed you? What have you done to cope with the consequences?

4. What kinds of important lifestyle decisions are you facing at this time in your life? Use the pattern outlines found in this chapter to help you discern God's call among your perceived options.

5. How do you handle the small decisions in everyday life? Are you sensitive to the movements of selfishness and love in these small decisions? Explain.

15 | Spirituality and Grace

Today's Catholic Church continues to convene various study groups, conferences, and synods to examine lay spirituality. Some of the early reports coming from these gatherings are rich in their analyses of the general needs of the laity. But is there such a thing as lay spirituality? Are lay people a different class of human beings with different spiritual needs than the professionally religious?

There is a tremendous variation in lifestyles that can be readily observed among the laity. They live in solitude or in faith-sharing communities, as married or divorced, with and without children, in free and oppressive political climates, and working at jobs they love or hate. They truly have a spirituality of their own, but it must be addressed in broad, general terms.

One of the better results of these reflections on lay spirituality is that it has stimulated intensive discussion concerning the very meaning of the term *spirituality*. In recent years, for example, the word *spiritual* has been used in a strictly secular sense as simple self-awareness, or getting in touch with a person's inner world, or struggling with the meaning of life. Modern magazines describe various workshops and retreats designed to "enhance spiritual growth" by teaching such techniques as astral travel, self-hypnosis, and communing with nature by dancing to the rhythm of bongo drums. This secular use of the word *spiritual* without reference to God can sometimes be very confusing. People try to explain this by saying that they themselves are spiritual but not religious; their explanations, are more bewildering than enlightening.

The traditional use of the term *spirituality* refers to an approach by means of which you become united with God. The many spiritualities found among the world religions have this much in common: They all attempt to influence humanity in the direction of its ultimate roots in God (or Ultimate Reality, as the case may be). All emphasize similar disciplines of prayer, study, and service, but that is where the similarities end. On examination of these spiritualities, it can be seen that they are clustered around basic beliefs concerning the nature of God, the nature of human beings, and God's expectations of human beings. But it is these belief systems that comprise what is called *religion*. It is religion that provides the dogmatic and ritualistic focus within which spiritualities lead people to God. This is why it is so difficult to understand what people mean when they say they are spiritual but not religious. How can a spirituality be lived out in a religious vacuum?

Within Christianity there are many spiritualities that, on the surface, appear to have very little in common. After further study, however, it can be seen that they have their common rootedness in the Gospel and Church teachings. Thus the Redemptorist, Franciscan, Benedictine, Carmelite, Ignatian, and other great spiritualities that have so enriched the Church all have a common Christian theme.

The spiritual living skills advocated in this book emphasize that Christian spirituality becomes effective if it helps to bring the functions of consciousness into their ultimate focus in

Christ. Any Christian spirituality will be effective to the extent that it includes something like the spiritual living skills outlined in this book. The reason: These living skills will deepen your surrender to God and increase your growth in love for others. To neglect any of these skills can be spiritually disastrous.

Pathways to Serenity can be used to develop a Christian spirituality as presented here or it can be combined with the renewal processes in which you are already engaged. When you keep in mind that the primary task of any Christian spirituality ought to be the transformation of human nature in the image of Christ, then the importance of spiritual living skills becomes apparent. It is by practicing and living out these skills daily that you bring all the functions of consciousness into submission in Christ. To neglect any of these skills is to stunt your Christian growth. If your present spiritual structure seems to incorporate all of these skills, then you can expect to grow eventually into the fullness of Christian maturity. If, however, your spirituality seems to be lacking in any of the areas described in this book, then it will surely be helpful to begin working on the living skills that have been neglected.

Now it is possible that some people may disagree with the notion of spiritual living skills. The most common objection is that it sounds like a spirituality of self-salvation by works rather than by grace. But it is precisely because of grace that spiritual living skills work so beautifully when practiced. It is the grace of God's call that turns your attention to these skills in the first place; applying these skills can be seen as your *response* to God's call. But even in this response there is grace, for the very efficacy of the skills is a grace. In searching for a comparison that pictures what actually happens, some religious teachers have described the process in the following manner: The spiritual living skills are sparked by God's own loving energy. As long as you keep in mind that everything is grace, there will be little danger of viewing this living-skills approach as an attempt at self-salvation.

This focus on spiritual living skills emphasizes a principle that has been confirmed hundreds of times in the lives of many. The principle here is that God will not impose upon you what you should do for yourself. While it is true that your entire existence would collapse were it not sustained by God's grace, it is also true that God has entrusted certain aspects of the creation to your own stewardship. Most specifically, your body and your consciousness belong to you, and God generally does not impose grace in these areas without your permission. This is not to say that God cannot override your willfulness: God can do anything! It is to say that your incarnational project requires a willing cooperation with grace in the development of your mind and body. In this context, spiritual living skills may be viewed as those practices that enable you to cooperate with God in the unfolding of your life in love.

When it comes to transforming human consciousness, God only stands at the door of the soul and knocks (see Revelation 3:20). Spiritual living skills are specific ways in which you open the doors of consciousness to allow God to come in and dine with you, and you with him. If you do not voluntarily open the door, however, he very seldom beats it down.

Reflection/Discussion/Questions

1. What kind of spirituality currently nourishes your growth in Christ?

2. How can the spiritual living skills presented in this book strengthen the spirituality you are currently living?

3. In your own words, write a few statements summarizing what you believe about the human condition, and the means by which persons are renewed in God. Compare your statement with the Twelve Steps of Alcoholics Anonymous, and the Pathways summary in Appendixes Two and Three.

4. How do you understand the role of grace in the spiritual life? How do you avoid falling into a spirituality of self-salvation?

PART THREE

Appendixes

APPENDIX ONE

Other Helpful
Spiritual Practices

Now that you have come to a better understanding of the relationship between your consciousness and your human needs and have studied the different spiritual living skills, this first appendix will treat various practical helps for living a truly spiritual life. It is suggested that you read a few of these reminders each night at bedtime or at a quiet break during the day, repeating them to yourself from time to time. These points concern eleven essential areas of your life.

I. Perspectives

1. One hundred years from now, your body shall lie rotting in a grave with the worms, and it is likely that 99.999999% of the world's population will not even know or care that you ever lived.

2. People of today are like voyagers on an ocean cruise who are busy partying, decorating their cabins, playing shuffleboard, and planning future trips when all the while the ocean liner is slowly sinking.

3. Nothing is forever except God. Your bad moods shall pass, and your difficult circumstances shall one day cease. Everything shall perish in the end; only God shall remain. What you have worried over shall be no more. Only that which is rooted in God shall persist.

4. The universe is God's farm, and the people of the world are all seeds of sorts, sown by God to ripen when the time is right.

5. There are five challenges you must face. If any are neglected, growth will be distorted.

- Love God above all else.
- Love others as yourself.
- Work hard, using your talents for good.
- Enjoy what you can when you can.
- Accept sufferings when they come and learn from them.

6. Life is loving, working, enjoying, and suffering,
    one day at a time,
        one moment at a time,
            in God's presence.

7. God is your joy, ever enough.
God is now, your joy is now.
Love is the way, peace is the guide.
Love now, live in the Lord.

II. Awareness

1. Are you at home? If not, then who is?

2. God is with you, loving you now. Receive, then, the courage to open your eyes and start moving!

3. In him you live and move and have your being. If you wish to see God, you need simply open your eyes.

4. Life means placing one foot in front of the other,
    walking on this earth.
One moment at a time,
    walking in eternity.

5. Take on a gentle, loving presence, now. (A consciousness focusing phrase.)

6. Do not project past or present joys and sorrows into the future. Leave the future open in hope, and you will remain in reality.

7. Miracles, miracles everywhere!
    Your smile, your face, the sun in your hair:
The stars at night, the ground under feet;
    The water you drink, the food that you eat;
Birds and sky and sea and breeze,

Lovers and children, flowers and trees.
Everywhere miracles: all around!
Open your heart, hear their sounds.

8. Just be here now with God; there's no need for a fixed agenda — this is always enough!

9. There is indeed such a thing as an error in judgment, but it is not so common as errors in awareness. Lapses in consciousness account for most traffic accidents, broken appointments, and keys locked inside cars.

10. Spiritual consciousness cannot be sustained so long as you retain ideas of win-or-else competitiveness, deservingness, pretentiousness, and ambition — all of which the powers of sin support.

11. Preoccupations are largely about fear. They absorb your time and make you unaware of reality.

12. Enlightenment does not mean that you will not ever get tired or discouraged — only that you will be aware in your tiredness and discouragement.

13. Ego awareness naturally moves toward pain. Eliminate pain — at least the mental/emotional kind — and awareness will become free to enjoy a larger reality.

III. Identity

1. Wherever you go, whatever you do, you stand for Christ.

2. The truly natural human being is the mystic. What most people call "natural" is really carnal perversion.

3. Lose yourself in love for *anything,* and you will find *something* for your self. Lose yourself in the love of God and you will find your essential self.

4. Self-reflection can help you to realize successes, pitfalls, and errors, but it cannot produce self-realization. To attempt realization through self-reflection is like a mirror gazing at itself.

5. Anything can be a pretense for the false self, but sham piety is the most dangerous of all. A false self can take on the trappings of religion and congratulate itself on having realized the Christ-self.

6. If you can't find yourself, don't just sit there waiting for self-realization. Get moving, and do what you're doing in loving awareness. It will come to you in action and movement.

7. You are not your thoughts, you are not your feelings, you are not even what you have been, nor what you imagine yourself to be. You are the one who is loved by God. You are the awareness of God's love for you.

8. The false self is a prison, where fear reigns supreme.

9. Investing energy in a pretense is like building a house in quicksand or a cardboard bridge over a river.

10. The nature and business of the Christ-self shall always remain hidden from those who still retain a sense of deservingness, sufficiency, and honor.

11. If you strive to live constantly in God's presence, you will not get lost as you go from one project to the next; for God will be your home and the integrity of your identity.

12. Apart from the life of the body, a toe is only a decaying piece of flesh. Attached to the body, it attains its true toeness by doing what a toe is supposed to do.

13. You have no real self outside of God. The self which you create and nurture apart from God is merely an illusion.

14. The truth is not "Christ lives in you," but "You live in Christ." He is not yours, you are his. You are the clay, he is the potter.

15. You are a brain cell in God's consciousness. Having awakened, you are now privileged to see as he sees, to love as he loves. The old cellular structure remains; the life within it is different. New wine, new wineskins!

16. In the small-self, feelings are reactive to "you" and "yours" in the narrowest sense. In the higher-self, feelings are responsive to "we" and "ours." In the no-self, there are no personal feelings — only a steady, serene compassion, which is bliss.

17. The Christ-self is awakened by Love, nurtured in Love, and expanded in Love. In Love it lives and moves and has its being.

18. Most people discover the love of God through the love of other people. The mystic, however, discovers love of others primarily through the love of God.

19. Use no adjectives in reference to yourself, for all are limiting. Instead, simply say: "I have gifts, I have weaknesses, I am loved!"

IV. The Experience of God

1. If God is experienced as an object of the self, there is the possibility that this object is merely the creation of the self. This is why in the purest experiences of God, there is no sense of self whatsoever. Rather, the self returns after the experience, vaguely aware that something mysterious has happened.

2. God is the force that binds together the fragments of your life into harmonious meaning and impels you to bond with others in love.

3. God is the essential core of all that exists. To empathize with anything in creation, then, is to experience something of God.

4. "Where is the ocean?" asks the fish. "Where is God?" inquires the intellectual. (Adapted from a proverb by Anthony de Mello.)

5. The experience of God is like the experience of water to a person who is floating within it.

6. God's presence is always new, yet familiar; extraordinary, yet common; fresh, yet aged.

7. You are like a sailboat. God is the wind and the sea. Sometimes the wind blows; sometimes the sea moves; at other times calmness prevails. Do not cling to intensity or calm, but allow the wind and sea to simply move you where they will.

8. "Those who know do not say, and those who say do not know" *(Tao te Ching)*. This statement brings home the utter futility of trying to fully describe the experience of God.

V. Discernment

1. If a feeling persists despite your surrender of its issues to Providence, it is probably pointing to an issue you need to work on.

2. The only sure thing about pleasant feelings is that you shall want them back when they are gone.

3. Use your common sense. (If, during prayer, you find yourself growing sleepy, it probably means that you are tired.)

4. Just because you have the opportunity to do something good does not mean that you should do it. Is it God's will?

5. Test your feelings before you analyze their roots. To move beyond feelings too quickly is to invite intellectual stagnation.

6. Do not evaluate your spiritual exercises under any other criteria than their ability to help you to love in this moment.

7. If you surrender yourself to God with the full intent of doing his will — however unpleasant it may be — you may rest assured that God has accepted your surrender and is even now drawing you in the direction you need to go.

8. Were you ever confused? In turmoil? If a person came to you in such a frame of mind, what would you recommend? Listen to your Inner Adviser for the answer.

9. The true mystic desires only to love others and leave them free. The false mystic speaks much of God, less of love, and very little of freedom.

10. Do you seek the will of God? You may say yes only if you are willing to do the hard thing.

11. When struggling with others in a conflict, ask: "Whose problem is whose?" Accept what is yours to work with and let go of the rest.

12. "Where there's a will, there's a way," reads an old adage. The question is: will to what? and which way?

13. Crooked means do not produce holy ends. Never!
Loving means produce kingdom ends. Always!

14. If loving brings about the destruction of certain matters, then those matters needed to be destroyed. (Adapted from a saying by Leo Tolstoy.)

15. If your purpose is to get rich or become famous, you may choose many avenues in pursuit of your goal. God, however, is in no way bound to show you the right way. If, however, you are striving to grow in virtue and you are open to God's will, then God is bound by his own promises to provide guidance and support.

16. Develop the habit of thinking before acting; it takes serious thought to form a judgment.

17. After surrendering everything to God in prayer, dream your dreams, ask your questions, and note your concerns.

18. Feelings teach the ego balance between the extremes that it may find its center and so become rooted in God. Contemplative prayer is the rooting.

19. In the now there are options; but choices are made in awareness on the basis of loving preferences — now this, later that. Who can plan such actions in advance? Who would want to? Go with the flow!

20. Beware the "project" of holiness or "attaining" virtue. These are attempts of the false self to expand its control into the arena of the spiritual.

21. Your human project is the most important of all, including your prayer, marriage, parenting, work, and even religious orientations. When making decisions, keep this large perspective in mind.

VI. Prayer

1. Theology is the recipe; prayer, the eating of the cake. It is much better to eat cake than it is to read recipes about how to make it (although there can be no cake without a recipe).

2. If you ever want to lose interest in ministry, all you have to do is stop praying.

3. Solitude, silence, and surrender: these constitute the essentials of contemplative prayer. Without all three, prayer will be shallow.

4. Prayer that does not change you is merely a resting in your own spirit. Beware the feeling of self-satisfaction because you have "prayed."

5. To pray with others is to allow the Trinity to become manifest among human beings.

6. In prayer, seek only to grow in the love and knowledge of God and you shall never be disappointed.

7. To say that the gift of tongues is "not for everyone" is to err grievously. Why should a prayer gift be only for some? And who does not need God's gifts? The gift of tongues may well be for many the key to opening up the spiritual life, because those who can surrender their tongues to God in prayer will quickly learn to surrender the whole of themselves.

8. Most people who say "everything I do is prayer" are people who know nothing about prayer, and who merely wish to excuse themselves from the discipline of prayer. There is no spirituality that will bear loving fruit without prayer. This is the witness of the saints and the masters.

9. Anything can be prayer if done in loving presence. You can be fed all day long! But this possibility is only for those who have become empty through surrender in "formal" prayer.

10. Are you confused and afraid? Does everything seem so superficial? On your knees, then; and don't get up until you know who you are!

11. It is true that prayer helps you to love, but such a pragmatic view is not the main justification for prayer. You pray because it is good that creatures commune with their Creator and find themselves in their Creator.

12. Place no constraints on what God wants to do through you and in you. In God, all things are possible.

13. In prayer, you confront the Spotless Mirror that reflects back to you who you really are. Prayer is thus the barometer that measures the quality of your life. Peaceful prayer reflects a peaceful lifestyle; turmoil encountered in prayer indicates a need for lifestyle changes.

14. Do not discuss your prayer with a spiritual director who does not pray or who is not as serious about prayer as you are. Such a person will distort your growth. It is much better to progress in prayer without spiritual direction than to submit yourself to a poor director.

15. Remember this about contemplative prayer:
> The wind blows the sails,
>> the vessel moves.
> The wind subsides,
>> the streams carry.
> The oarsmen rest.

VII. Honesty

1. What God wants most in this world is a heart that is open to receiving his gifts, for he gives lavishly for the pure pleasure of seeing people become joyful. Such is the nature of his love, and the main impediments to receiving his gifts are feelings of self-sufficiency and deservingness and a desire to control everything.

2. Honesty — what an absolute value! If anything is to happen, you must be honest about everything — at least to yourself. Offer no pretense; practice frankness instead. Freed by truth, you are forgiven by love.

3. "An idiot is someone who does not know what you yourself learned only five minutes ago." This is the way a proud person speaks.

4. If you think you are better than others, it is because you have forgotten about your pride and selfishness. The saint, who is relatively free of pride, looks upon others not in judgment but in compassion, aware of the bondage that grace has transformed.

5. Pretentious piety is an abomination. It is far better to say nothing about your beliefs than to be proud that you have shared them.

6. Banish the word *deserve* from your vocabulary. You are not saved because you "deserve" heaven, but because you have accepted it as gift.

7. It is true that you stand for Christ in all that you do. But you are not his credibility. Honesty in imperfection is much more pleasing to God than a pretense of perfection "for the sake of Christ."

8. The starting point in the spiritual life is "I am nothing, God is everything." Beware those so-called gurus who forget this truth.

9. It is impossible for people to attain God by "trying," because their very act of "trying" is precisely the reason they do not attain God.

10. Nature abhors a vacuum. A heart that has surrendered all self-will shall draw into its emptiness the very heart of God.

11. When feeling grandiose, take out a biology book and contemplate the structure of a kidney or an eyeball or the citric acid cycle. Did you design these things?

VIII. Detachment

1. Let go (emotionally) of everything you cannot handle. Focus your energy only on what is in your power to handle now.

2. Prefer no other reality than now. Choose to do nothing more than what reality calls you to do now in the service of love. Do this and you will live in serenity.

3. If your desires conflict with the demands of reality, you had better adjust, or else you will be filled with resentment toward the cause of the conflict.

4. God gives each person a share of the Cross to teach human powerlessness and the utter futility of carnal attachments.

5. Interfere in the lives of others only out of love for them. It is a dangerous thing to tamper with destiny.

6. Strike a powerful blow against your vanity by doing something kind for others — without letting them or anyone else know about it.

7. "God is free to do his own will on his own level when my heart, being disinterested, is bent on neither this nor that" (Meister Eckhart).

8. Relax! God is looking after the world and your own life even while you sleep and when you pray.

9. You must even let go of the consequences of your actions. Nothing that you have done is so bad that it cannot be forgiven, and even good works can become corrupted. Keep moving forward. Don't look back.

10. People are miserable because they want what they cannot have or what they should not have. Put to death all desiring save for an increase in love and you will be happy.

IX. Faith

1. You do not know all the possibilities and probabilities of life. Therefore, you might as well believe that God does.

2. Nothing can really hurt you, except despairing of God's love. Even suffering and death have been brought into the divine economy.

3. You say you believe in God. Even the devil believes as much. But do you believe in a good God, who is already intimately involved in your life?

4. Faith does not bring God into your soul, but opens your awareness to the Lord who has always been there. God does not *come* to you; he has never *left* you.

5. You already have everything you need for doing what you must do in this moment. (A consciousness focuser.)

6. Christ is risen; the ultimate victory is assured; God will save the world. Your fearful vigilance is merely wasted energy.

7. Do you believe that God's will is your happiness? If not, then whose will is?

8. The absence of God is only a feeling, not a metaphysical truth. Know that God is with you even when your feelings do not sense this.

9. With faith there is no reason to fear death. Resurrection awaits the faithful.

10. On an experiential level, faith is that quality of awareness that is alert to God's connection with the self and all of creation. Because this quality of awareness is not merely manufactured by the ego, it is called *supernatural*.

X. Knowledge

1. The spiritually awakened mind is none other than the ordinary, everyday mind, but free from all anxiety and illusions of separateness. In such a mind, all knowledge is seen in the context of love. This is wisdom.

2. The environment can influence thoughts and beliefs. Therefore, the environment is extremely important!

3. To know and not to do is not yet to know. Instead, it is mental paralysis.

4. Human culture is ultimately an expression of mind. If there are problems with these cultures, it is because there are problems in the minds that created them.

5. Mystical consciousness cannot be sustained in a mind that tries to manipulate truth for its own ends. This is why honesty is one of the absolute values.

6. Theology is the map; spirituality is the road; life is the journey.

7. Life is an experience to be lived, not a problem to be solved.

8. When you have progressed in theological knowledge to the point where few burning questions remain, you can be sure that the time has arrived to turn more seriously to the journey inward.

9. To truly understand something, you must stand under it, or empathize with it. Therefore, empathy is the highest form of knowledge; contemplative prayer is the most exalted human experience.

10. Thoughts, beliefs, and convictions: these must, finally, direct your life. But allow yourself to experience God in as many modes as possible — music, conversation, human love, bodily sensations, prayer, play, aesthetic delights, and so forth. Surrender yourself fully in each of these modes, knowing that they all teach something about God.

11. You learn nothing by experience. You learn only through reflecting on experience.

12. "Yes, but . . . " Is this what you always say of your God-concept or your ideas of another person or, indeed, about anything? There is an inherent danger in labels, in that they become substitutes for reality.

13. What makes a good idea good is its power to move you to serenity and integration without depriving others of their legitimate needs. A bad idea produces the opposite effects.

14. The undefiled creation (a world not manipulated by human beings) is a partial reflection of the consciousness of God. To know creation is to know something about God. Even so, God's innermost nature cannot be known except through God's self-revelation. This is the meaning of Christ: Persons who know Christ know God's inner nature and their own nature as well.

XI. Love

1. Love is being and doing at the same time. In love, all dualisms are dissolved.

2. To be committed to another in awareness, honesty, and benevolence: This is the best way to love.

3. Love without empathy is do-goodism, which is ultimately a form of pride. If you cannot love people, then leave them alone!

4. If you desire anything other than love for another, you can eventually justify any imaginable cruelty toward this person while invoking your principles as justification.

5. Listen, clarify, empathize, affirm.

Listen, clarify, empathize, affirm.

Listen, clarify, empathize, affirm.

Only after doing so may you confront and negotiate.

6. Contact with another is an opportunity to increase love and strengthen the Church.

7. The Church lives by love. Every time you extend yourself in love, the life of God enters into the process to join wayward cells together in ever-novel and extraordinarily beautiful arrangements.

8. What should you do around people? Love them. Who manages best around people? A lover.

9. "But what does it mean to be a lover?" you ask. Spend your life with this question and you shall have passed your time very well.

10. You can love others without liking them, although it is much better to do both. It seems that Jesus did not particularly like pompous and self-righteous people. Still, there can be no doubt that he loved them — that he extended himself to relate with them in a manner that would lead them to growth.

11. An open heart is the wellspring of love.

12. Love goes on and on and on . . .

Like a river it flows,

Always present, always new.

13. God loves you all the time. That is the witness of Christ. Believe nothing else about God and you shall have grasped the heart of the Gospel.

14. The closed heart and the narrow mind — these are the primary obstacles to the working of the Spirit. These, too, are the primary characteristics of the small-self.

15. That which you love in yourself and about yourself you shall also love in others. This is why the first great commandment is to love God above all. When you love God thus, you are grasped by God, and you know that others, too, belong to God.

16. In the last analysis, there is no conflict between love of God, self, and neighbor. Love is one.

17. Self-love is different from selfishness in that self-love means looking after your legitimate needs in gratitude for God's gifts, and in such a manner as not to hurt yourself and others — all with a view of returning to others with richer blessings to share. In other words, self-love is open to love relationships; selfishness remains closed against them.

18. The deepest love is not possible without complete self-forgetfulness — not of the dependent kind, where you give up self to cling to the other, but of the transcendent kind, where you annihilate self in complete identification with the other.

19. Listen: You can never *receive* enough of anything to fill the depths of your being and satisfy your deepest hungers for security, pleasure, and peace. It is only *in giving* of self that you will receive what you need in these areas.

20. Love is also a willingness to receive the gifts of others, that you might be joined with them and allow them to experience the joy of giving. No receivers, no givers.

21. If, for one second, you are not moved with compassion for those who are hurting, but instead feel a sense of superiority toward them, it means that your small-self is yet intact, and you'd best plead for mercy and the grace to love your brothers and sisters in Christ.

22. Capacity for empathy is the surest sign of spiritual health, for empathy presupposes the internal emptiness in which the divine fullness may rest.

Pathways Spirituality: A Summary

What It Is

1. All persons have needs, and all persons seek to meet them. The most common ones are the physical (needs of the body) and psychological (esteem, security, status, and power).

2. Human consciousness is primarily oriented toward the gratification of wants/needs. Consciousness consists of your ability to perceive, consider, feel, decide, and act. The ego is the volitional center of consciousness.

3. The manner in which you meet your needs makes you either more selfish/separate/fragmented/fearful or more loving/united/whole/fearless.

4. Spiritual living skills enable you to meet your needs in a loving manner because they focus the functions of consciousness in the will of God. These skills include the following:

- **Right behavior** helps you avoid loose speech, over-indulgence in food/drink, illicit sex, stealing and all forms of dishonesty, and violence. It implies the practice of the corporal and spiritual works of mercy.
- **Right desires** urge the practice of renunciation of cravings that lead to wrong behaviors. You should encourage benevolent desires toward all people and creation.
- **Right use of feelings** means that you accept all feelings without judgment, express them appropriately, and learn from them.
- **Right beliefs** induce you to commit to memory healthy thoughts about God, human nature, and life's meaning.

- **Right values** teach you how to meet your needs in a loving manner through humility, prudence, justice, courage, and moderation.
- **Right awareness** reminds you to let go of the past, trust in the future, and live in the now of God's presence.
- **Right discernment** gives you guidelines for making loving decisions.

How to Live It

1. Pray in the mornings — at least twenty minutes. Place emphasis on surrender to God.
2. Live your daily life in honesty, awareness, and benevolence. "Do what you're doing in truth and love."
3. Make a consciousness examen for fifteen minutes in the evening. Start with prayer. Examine your day.

- What did you do?
- How did you feel?
- What do your feelings teach you about beliefs/motives?
- Affirm the good, ask pardon for failures.
- In imagination, relive troublesome situations. See and feel yourself acting in a loving manner, using the necessary living skills.
- Thank God for the day and rest assured of God's love for you.

Pathways Spirituality:
Its Psycho-spiritual Dynamics

1. Where total surrender to the requirements of love is lacking, there is fear, resentment, guilt, and other forms of emotional pain.

2. Where there is emotional pain, there is self-concern.

3. Where there is self-concern, there is an ego, a framed center of consciousness designed to fend off further threat and solve the problems of concern.

4. Where there is an ego, there is a narcissistic pole in consciousness. When behavior proceeds from this pole, there will be an increase in separateness, fragmentation — in short, sin.

5. When your life fluctuates between points one and four of the above, there is addiction. When identity comes to rest in this cycle, there is hell.

6. Where there is an ego, there is also a spiritual pole, an opening to love, relationships, and wholeness. Moving toward this spiritual pole will require a renunciation of the demands of the narcissistic pole and the identification with another center of consciousness — for the Christian: Christ.

7. The way to move the ego away from selfishness to love is through prayer and the practice of spiritual living skills. The Holy Spirit assists you in living out these skills.

8. Growth proceeds through a spiritually oriented ego until, finally, the ego itself becomes absorbed in Christ. When this happens, the narcissistic pole is practically silenced, although there ever remains the possibility of making a selfish choice and so reverting back to point one.

Pathways Support Group

Individuals interested in starting a support group are encouraged to read *How to Form a Christian Growth Support Group* (Liguori Publications, 1985). This booklet was written with Twelve-Step groups in mind, but its guidelines for facilitators and its Twelve Traditions for group life apply very well to a group of this type.

Format

1. Gathering: Allow about 10 minutes for people to settle in; have refreshments, books, and handouts ready.

2. Prayer: This may simply be a song, followed by quiet; psalms, liturgy of the hours, and other prayer forms also work well; charismatic groups may simply opt for spontaneous prayer (5-10 minutes).

3. Scripture: Read one or two Scripture passages for the coming Sunday; alternative passages may also be used (5 minutes).

4. Study or Sharing Time: This is the main body of the meeting. It is suggested that meetings occasionally feature a teaching (study), but that sharing be the group staple (30-45 minutes).

A. Share group questions:

- What passages in the Scriptures spoke to you? How did they challenge you?

- Relate a recent struggle or joy you have experienced. What have you learned from this?
- With which of the Pathways living skills have you been struggling lately? Ask for feedback from group members on how they understand and live out these principles.

B. Study times might include the following:

- A teaching on the Scriptures for the coming Sunday and how they relate to spiritual growth.
- A teaching on one or two chapters from this book.
- Reading a chapter of this book in the group, then discussing the questions at the end of the chapter.
- Reading a section of "Other Helpful Spiritual Practices" from this book, then discussing how group members understand these principles in their lives.

5. Prayer: This provides time to pray for one another's needs. Join hands, make a circle, voice petitions and thanksgiving aloud. Conclude with the Lord's Prayer or Glory Be.

6. Business: Here announcements are made about future meetings, dues, newsletters, and so forth.

7. Refreshments and fellowship.

Training Opportunities

Parishes and other communities seeking workshops and training in Pathways spiritual principles and/or support group formation will find help from Personal Growth Services, Inc., 13586 Neil Avenue, Baton Rouge, LA 70810, (504) 766-7615. Support groups are encouraged to register their existence at this address to receive newsletters and other helpful aids.

Notes on Christian Cosmic Consciousness

The state of Cosmic Consciousness represents the highest level of spiritual growth. It is a possibility for all; however, it is attained by only a few. It is also misunderstood by many, who assume that it refers to some far-out altered state of mind with no relevance to the everyday affairs of the "real world." Because of these common preconceptions and the tremendous interest people have in this state when properly explained, here are a few notes based on the writings of mystics, the research of human developmental scientists, and the personal experiences of the writer.

General Characteristics of the Cosmic State
(in comparison with Adult state and Conscientious state)

1. There is a "softening" of ego boundaries; the self-limiting wall of ego defenses has broken down.

- The personality is no longer focused and held together by selfish desires and cravings. Instead, personal awareness has to do with your relationship to the whole, that is, to various levels of community — family, Church, nation, and most importantly, the entire world.
- Personal security is no longer based on being well defended, but derives from the awareness that you are well loved.

2. Most major Shadow issues have been resolved. Any emotional pain experienced is from daily issues. These daily pains are not complicated by attachment to unresolved issues from the past.

- You become acutely sensitized to emotional pain in yourself and others because there are no longer protective ego defenses.
- You become aware of the tremendous varieties of pain confronting people in everyday living.
- Genuine empathy and compassion become a real possibility for the first time.

3. There are temptations to selfish behavior, but these are seen clearly as separating forces, and they are easily resisted (although occasional slips do take place).

- Narcissistic self-consciousness has been annihilated. No longer does the narcissistic self have its "big nose" in everything.

4. There is a breakdown in dualistic thinking — either/or, win/lose, and so forth. Thinking becomes holistic; the truth is recognized in terms of the good of the whole.

5. Far from being an altered state, it feels quite common and mundane. There are fewer emotional highs and lows. Instead, there is a serene, compassionate readiness to enjoy or to endure.

- There is no longer a sense of enmity between body, mind, conscience, memory, and other members of the soul. You experience yourself as a simple whole. In this state, the body is no impediment to Spirit. Indeed, you discover that to be human means to live fully in the body.
- There is complete freedom to do with the body and mind whatever you wish (within the framework of natural laws, of course). If you want to think, you may think; if you wish to stop thinking, you may do so and withdraw into

silence. Conscious awareness has become the captain of the soul. The members of the soul now obey their ruler.

6. You must still study to learn, evaluate options when making decisions, and struggle to love others. There is no infallible knowledge — no bypassing the ordinary means of learning. The only difference is that you engage in these activities in the awareness of being part of a greater whole.

7. Prayer in this state is essentially contemplative. All willfulness in prayer becomes distasteful. Only a resolute passivity in God's presence satisfies.

- Although complete emptiness of self-will in God's presence is seldom attainable, it is the goal of this prayer.
- God is no longer experienced as an object of the ego's attention, but as the very ground of your life. You are simply in God, moving with God, participating with God in everything. All dialogue with God takes place in this awareness.
- Cognitive approaches to relating with God become distasteful and unfulfilling.
- This loss of a felt sense of God is quite confusing at first, then later becomes enjoyable.
- The importance of a sound, theological vision to help you understand how God operates is essential.

8. In relating with others, there is still the possibility of rejection, disappointment, and hurt.

- Because the self is now solidly rooted in God, however, setbacks in relationships are not personally devastating.
- There is a genuine freedom to love in this state, for you are not dependent on others' approval.

9. You know yourself to be a qualitatively different person than you were in previous ego states.

- .Although different, there is appreciation for the continuity of the journey — how it was all necessary to lead to this point.
- You may assess the consciousness of earlier ego states through contemplative remembering, although this usually proves distasteful. There is no desire to go back; the past is dead.
- Just as parents recognize and respect children in their limited ego development, so do you in Cosmic Consciousness respect those who are not yet done with the Shadow. In fact, lack of respect here is a sure indication that you are not in the Cosmic state, but, instead, in a Persona role trying to act the part.

10. You do not enter the Cosmic state all at once — as you might enter another geographic place. As with other ego states, it emerges slowly; you experience it at first for a few minutes a day — perhaps after a period of deep prayer. Later, you may live this way for several hours a day. After a while, it becomes the only way you wish to experience life. It is then that the last pitched battle with the Shadow begins in earnest. This is the Dark Night of the Soul.

Essential Conditions for Cosmic Consciousness

There are four:
1. A sound grasp of spiritual living skills.
2. Contemplative prayer.
3. Willingness to deal responsibly with your internal pain.
4. A sound theology based on right beliefs to support you when feelings no longer guide the way.

Suggested Reading

This book represents the fruit of fifteen years of spiritual reading, study, and discernment. There are so many writers and so many books that have influenced me that it would be impossible to list them all. Nevertheless, I shall mention some of the books that have been most helpful in stimulating my growth along one or more of the pathways outlined in this book.

First and foremost, I must mention the works of Thomas Merton. *Zen and the Birds of Appetite* (New Directions, 1968) helped to clarify some of the cloudier issues concerning the small-self and the Christ-self (although Merton uses different terminology). His writings on prayer, nuclear war, and what it means to be a Christian in this age have also been helpful to me. James Finley's book about Merton, *Merton's Palace of Nowhere* (Ave Maria Press, 1978), is also, in my opinion, a must for anyone seriously committed to growth in Christ.

The books and tapes of Father John Powell, S.J. (Argus Communications), have been helpful to me in my growth in self-worth, communication skills, and sharing feelings. In particular, I recommend *The Secret of Staying in Love* and *Why Am I Afraid to Tell You Who I Am?* Father Powell's books are also most helpful in pointing out the critical role of beliefs as seen in *Fully Human, Fully Alive* and *The Christian Vision*.

Twelve Step literature is usually published and distributed by the various recovery groups. My own book, *Becoming a New Person* (Liguori, 1984), offers an introduction to the Steps from a Christian standpoint. I also recommend the literature of the recovery groups, however. This body of writing, "nonprofessional" though it may be, is very rich in its grasp of the human condition and its spiritual needs.

If you sense a need for a few books to challenge you to service (the Christian meaning of status), try *Dare to Be Christian* by Bernard Häring (Liguori Publications, 1983). *The Faith That Does Justice,* edited by John Haughey (Paulist Press, 1977), is also sure to disturb your complacency. So will *His Way,* by David Knight, S.J. (St. Anthony Messenger Press, 1973), and *The Cost of Discipleship,* by Dietrich Bonhoeffer (Macmillan, 1963). The social encyclicals of the Catholic Church are also challenging, though rather dry.

Without prayer, your spiritual life will be fruitless. In this age, Rev. Thomas Greene has emerged as one of the great teachers on prayer. Ave Maria Press offers three of his books on the topic: *Opening to God; When the Well Runs Dry;* and *Weeds Among the Wheat.* My own book, *Praying the Daily Gospels* (Ave Maria Press, 1984), can provide a springboard for daily meditation. So can *Growing in Inner Freedom* (Liguori, 1986), a booklet which in many ways complements this present work.

Also on the subject of prayer, I am pleased to recommend an exciting new book that I came across after this work was nearly completed. It is entitled *Biospirituality: Focusing as a Way to Grow* (Loyola University Press, 1985). Authors Peter Campbell and Edwin McMahon present a contemplative process called focusing, which helps you to tap the inner bodily wisdom that most people seem to ignore. It is an important book, with tremendous implications for cultivating right awareness, right use of feelings, and right discernment. Dr. Eugene Gendlin's book, *Focusing* (Bantam, 1981), would be a wonderful complement to Campbell and McMahon's book.

Those who struggle with the heavier metaphysical questions ought to get to know the works of John Haught. His *Cosmic Adventure* (Paulist Press, 1984) and *What Is God?* (Paulist Press, 1986) address difficult metaphysical questions head-on. Karl Rahner and Herbert Vorgrimler's *Dictionary of Theology* (Crossroad, 1981) also takes on numerous difficult issues.

Beliefs about God, human nature, and the meaning of life play a pivotal role in life. The above works and books like Claude Tresmontant's *Christian Metaphysics* (Sheed and Ward, 1965), Robert Faricy's *Teilhard de Chardin's Theology of the*

Christian in the World (Sheed and Ward, 1967), and my own books, *Faith and Doubt Today* (Liguori Publications, 1985) and *Jesus on the Cross: Why?* (Ave Maria Press, 1987) can help you to grow in your Christian vision.

My presentation on ego states and growth trajectories represents a simplified summary of several rather technical works as well as reflection on my own experiences. Readers interested in going deeper here ought to read *Spiritual Development: An Interdisciplinary Approach,* by Daniel Helminiak (Loyola University Press, 1987). Also worth studying is James Fowler's *Stages of Faith: The Psychology of Human Development and the Quest for Meaning* (Harper and Row, 1981). For a Jungian perspective on spiritual growth, I highly recommend *From Image to Likeness: A Jungian Path in the Gospel Journey,* by my good friend Harold Grant (with Magdala Thompson and Thomas Clarke, Paulist Press, 1983). These three books will point readers to other stimulating works on various types of human growth patterns.

No matter how much you read, however, there is simply no substitute for spiritual experience. Without spiritual experience, reading all of the above books will not bear much fruit. If, however, these books inspire you to join a share group or a Life in the Spirit Seminar or to make a retreat or become faithful to daily prayer, they will have accomplished a very good thing.

OTHER BOOKS BY PHILIP ST. ROMAIN

GROWING IN INNER FREEDOM
A Guide for Today
Using Jesus Christ as a model of spiritual freedom and based on lessons found in the Scriptures, this book contains forty tested practices designed to help readers develop and nurture life-enriching attitudes. Individual topics include often overlooked — but very important — practices like: "Go the Extra Mile," and "Don't Worry Uselessly." **$1.95**

FAITH AND DOUBT TODAY
Personal Responses to Spiritual Struggles
This book comes as a result of the author's own struggle to grow in faith at a time when faith does not come easily. It discusses four sources of doubt with which most adult Christians must come to grips. Includes questions for reflection/discussion. **$3.25**

CATHOLIC ANSWERS TO FUNDAMENTALISTS' QUESTIONS
These pages contain clear, accurate answers to a great many questions that sincere Christians ask about the Catholic Church. The book covers six main areas of faith and practice, and was written for Catholics as well as questioning fundamentalists. **$1.95**

BECOMING A NEW PERSON
12 Steps to Christian Growth
Based on the same twelve-step plan used to free people from obsessive-compulsive behavior, this book offers "healthy" people a way to break free in their spiritual lives. A practical, easy-to-understand program for any Christian seeking personal fulfillment. **$2.95**

HOW TO FORM A CHRISTIAN GROWTH SUPPORT GROUP
A manual for **Becoming a New Person,** this book helps readers get a Christian Growth Support Group started. These pages explain what a group is, how to organize one, and what takes place at meetings. **$2.95**

Order from your local bookstore or write to:
Liguori Publications
Box 060, Liguori, Missouri 63057-9999
*(Please add $1.00 for postage and handling for orders
under $5.00; $1.50 for orders over $5.00.)*